WILL THE FUTURE WORK?

WILL THE FUTURE WORK?

Values for emerging patterns of work and employment

Howard Davis
David Gosling

World Council of Churches, Geneva

We gratefully acknowledge the support of the Department of Ministry and Mission, Church of Scotland, and members of the Society, Religion and Technology Project committee.

We also thank Dr F. Moghbeli of the Computer Services Unit, Glasgow College of Technology, for invaluable help in the preparation of this book, and Peter L. Tibbetts and Veronica Vaz for further assistance.

Cover design: Michael Dominguez/WCC

ISBN 2-8254-0842-5
© 1985 World Council of Churches, 150 route de Ferney, 1211 Geneva 20, Switzerland

Typeset by Thomson Press (India) Ltd
Printed in Switzerland

Contents

INTRODUCTION vii

PART I: TECHNOLOGY AND THE FUTURE OF WORK
Global Trends in Employment: Problems and Strategies
Theodor Leuenberger 3
Chips and Robots *Bruce Williams* 17
The Future of the Mixed Economy *David Simpson* . . . 28

PART II: CURRENT EMPLOYMENT POLICIES AND ASSUMPTIONS
A View from Industry *John Davidson* 41
Labour and New Technology: a New Strategy *Lynne Amery* 45
Labour Market Planning: the Role of a State Agency *Robert Whyte* 54
International Perspectives: the European Community *Marc Lenders*. 60
International Perspectives: Malaysia's Electronics Industry
Stephen Maxwell 66

PART III: AN ALTERNATIVE WORK ETHIC?
Employment and the Theology of Work *David Bleakley*. 73
Work Ideologies: Prospects for Participation *Peter Cressey*. 86
Towards a Normative Work Ethic *Göran Collste* . . . 94

PART IV: CONCLUSIONS
Tasks for the Churches 103
1. Industrial Communities in Decline 103
2. The Social Impact of New Technologies. 106
3. Youth, Education and Training. 109
4. International Strategies 115

vi *Will the Future Work?*

PARTICIPANTS 119

BIBLIOGRAPHY 122

AUTHORS 123

Introduction

This book is a contribution to our understanding of the future of work in the industrialized countries. The great challenge for those countries, particularly in western Europe, is to grasp the essential economic and social processes which are shaping the future of work and employment.

The following chapters are based on contributions to an international workshop on technology, employment and rapid social change, held in Glasgow, Scotland, from 10–14 September 1984. The workshop was jointly sponsored by the Church and Society Sub-unit of the World Council of Churches and the Church of Scotland's Society, Religion and Technology Project. By bringing together representatives of industry, trade unions, education, state and voluntary agencies and the churches, an opportunity was given for reflection on the foundations of a Christian understanding of work and employment in the light of present-day trends and policies. The central question was: How can the churches evaluate and make informed and practical responses to the problems and opportunities created by emerging patterns of work?

It has been rightly pointed out that for each generation, ecumenical social thinking has a different agenda, since it is always reflecting human situations. For two decades or more, "justice", "participation" and "sustainability" have been major themes in ecumenical reflection on economic and social questions. Their importance became clear in the 1960s when turbulence and change were sweeping every continent. The western capitalist countries had experienced their longest economic boom in history and were beginning to feel the negative consequences both in their cultures and in the deterioration of their physical environments. Certain socialist countries were beginning to experiment with market mechanisms, and liberation struggles were transforming many less developed parts of the world. On a global scale, it was apparent that the patterns of economic growth which had prevailed in the most developed countries, if pursued indefinitely, would lead to the exhaustion of the planet's finite resources and that these patterns were only possible through exploitation of people and resources in other parts of the world.

The need for justice in economic and political relations gained in urgency as colonialism was superseded by new relationships shaped by international capital and transnational corporations. The notion of sustainability was developed through consideration of the limitations of finite resources, and, on a smaller scale, through experiments with appropriate and ecologically responsible technologies. The need for participation by those caught up in the processes of change was seen as a prerequisite for any alternative strategies.

During the 1980s, however, the themes of cultural and political revolution and the need to restrain growth have become strangely anachronistic. With the world economic recession the burning questions again have to do with how we can create wealth and employment and stimulate growth. These questions are particularly pressing for the industrial economies of north and western Europe which are experiencing levels of unemployment unknown for more than thirty years. In the UK, where the workshop participants met, the official figure for registered unemployed is 3.25 million (13.4 per cent) and still rising. Vacancies exist for only one in seven unemployed claimants and even this dismal picture obscures the fact that there are many areas which have youth unemployment of well over 50 per cent. In 12 of the "travel-to-work" areas in Scotland, for example, the average unemployment rate is over 20 per cent.

Although the rate of unemployment in Britain continues to be dramatically higher than in most other major industrial countries, the problems are not unique. In fact, the UK, and Scotland in particular, can be seen as a striking example of the problem of decline and restructuring of employment which is affecting virtually all the western industrialized countries. There is acute social dislocation and deprivation, especially in the heartlands of primary industrial production based on coal mining, steelmaking, shipbuilding and manufacturing. As firms close or pursue greater efficiency through automation, traditional skills are rendered useless, school-leavers find their education terminates in a life of emptiness and frustrated opportunity, older workers face redundancy or early retirement and part-time workers struggle to survive with declining wages. Countless individuals and communities have been ravaged by these changes which they cannot control and often cannot anticipate. For many of those who have employment, the quality of working life has deteriorated and the defence mechanisms of trade union organizations have been seriously undermined. What is at stake is not only the future of these communities. In the long term, the social and spiritual as well as the economic wellbeing of the societies in which they are situated is threatened because unemployment is a denial of citizenship and the right to participate in the life of society.

Part of the difficulty which faces the churches or any other group wishing to intervene on behalf of the victims of this profound realignment of economic and social relationships is to correctly discern what is occurring and to understand what it will lead to. The efforts of a vast army of researchers, analysts and commentators are directed towards this end, but the results are unhappily contradictory and obscure. There is no general agreement that the long-term future will mean levels of employment higher or lower than in the past. On the one hand, the propensity to seek paid employment does not appear to have diminished and the wage-labour system which the western capitalist countries use to allocate labour to the productive process shows no sign of being replaced. On the other hand, the possibilities for labour-saving technologies appear to have increased dramatically with the "micro-electronics revolution". There are few grounds for firm predictions about new areas of economic activity, for example in the service sector, which might be labour-creating. Public sector employment, which more than compensated for the contraction of manufacturing employment in the 1960s, is unlikely to play the same role in the future. Indeed, office automation will probably result in reduced demand for workers in this sector. In many countries economic planning does little to reduce this uncertainty about the future of employment because it has very short-run objectives, especially when it is governed by laissez-faire, liberal market doctrines. What is certain is that the era of large-scale employment in a small range of primary industries is drawing to an end in the developed countries because basic manufacturing and assembly processes can be highly mechanized, and there is every economic incentive for this to happen. The debate about the future of work and employment has therefore come to focus on the employment impact of new technologies, especially those which are based on the microprocessor or "silicon chip".

The present impact of new technology on employment is the result of tendencies which are by no means new (mechanization of tasks, transfer of skills from workers to machines, stricter work discipline, etc.). What distinguishes this generation of "new technology" from earlier waves of innovation is the speed and intensity of these changes. Virtually every area of production and consumption is affected in one way or another because of the rapid decline in the cost of information processing with small and reliable devices. It is tempting, because of this widespread impact, to think of the "micro-revolution" as a great wave driving everything before it. Indeed some commentators write in terms which foster this image and the exaggerated optimism or pessimism which it tends to encourage. The optimists envisage a golden age of leisure. The pessimists see this same "leisure" as the denial of basic human rights. In reality, the impact, however great, is not one-dimensional. New technology does have a close relationship to levels of employment and patterns of working life whether in the factory, the office or the home. But this relationship does not exist apart from in an economic, social and cultural system which has a shaping influence on the technology itself. The technology is part of employment reduction as well as employment creation.

One of the effects of the global economic recession has almost certainly been to soften the employment-reducing impact of new technology because low investment and stagnant output are not conducive to innovation. The foreseeable future is likely to intensify the employment-reducing tendencies in manufacturing and, more dramatically, speed the advance of automation into much white-collar and professional work. Thus, however optimistic may be the projections about future economic growth and increase in demand for goods and services, there is unlikely to be significant employment growth in most industrial capitalist countries in the next five years without deliberate strategies for public sector employment creation, reduction and reorganization of working hours, work sharing, etc.

In the light of these pessimistic but reliable forecasts for employment to the end of the decade, it is surprising how persistent is the view that unemployment, poverty and social injustice are but temporary setbacks on the road to economic recovery. The fact that mass unemployment tends to create passivity, compliance and even fatalism, and that there is a lack of economic coordination and political will at the international level, combine to prevent the much-needed exploration of alternatives. The deep divisions in the industrial countries with high unemployment are being allowed to deepen further when the priority should be to set goals for the kind of society in which "good work" is available for all. As the bankruptcy of current "solutions" to unemployment, inflation and stagnation is revealed, these questions must find a way onto the agenda of policy-makers in government, industry, commerce, trade unions and education. They must not remain on the fringes of public debate.

From the end of the second world war through to the late 1970s there was a commitment by all major political parties in Europe to full employment. The increasingly high levels of unemployment in the late 1970s brought fears that the political system was being placed under intolerable strain by social deprivation on such a scale. Memories of the 1930s were revived and parallels drawn between then and now. In the event, the repercussions have not shaken the political foundations of western democracy and full employment has been shelved with scarcely a murmur. If anything, the effects of the economic recession have strengthened the hand of those political parties which seek to impose stricter industrial discipline, lower wages and to free labour markets from their current "restrictions". Some see this, then, not as the 1930s revisited but as a return to values and economic ideas of an earlier period of untramelled market capitalism.

The way ahead for work and employment is therefore unlikely to be determined by a head-on political struggle between labour and capital. The trade union movements in most European countries have been profoundly weakened by the pressures of the last ten years and the power base of the socialist and labour parties has been undermined. This weakness has affected the collectivist values and corporatist assumptions which these movements elaborated in the boom years of economic growth, the welfare state and consensus politics. The traditional values of solidarity and cooperation have lost their vitality and the vacuum created has been filled by more individualistic orientations based on consumption and life-style rather than production.

As far as it is possible to discern—and it is unlikely that we could ever have a clear perception of the end of an era even if we assume that we are living through one—the changes taking place in the sphere of work and employment amount to a significant realignment of the divisions of labour in society. Certainly it is easier to describe what we are leaving behind than what we are moving towards. While there is as much useful work to be done as there ever has been, the most powerful institutions of employment creation, namely large corporations and the state, are in a time of retreat or retrenchment. The changing international division of labour means that labour-intensive activities are more likely to be carried out in the newly-industrialized and developing countries, rather than in the old industrial countries of western Europe where labour costs are relatively high. Employment in the public sector has also reached the end of a phase of rapid expansion and is coming under increasing pressure from budgetary policies and new technology.

The resulting unemployment or underemployment (because part-time working has become more widespread) is creating a widening division between those with access to regular skilled work usually with large institutional employers and those with fewer opportunities for access to regular paid employment and careers. This latter group consists of the self-employed, unskilled and part-time workers whose "careers" are more sporadic and subject to circumstances over which they have little or no control. While this process of polarization describes the relative movement of groups in the market for wage labour, there is increasing evidence that the polarity extends to other types of work—in the "informal economy" within households, voluntary work, etc. Prof. Ray Pahl concludes a detailed study of work strategies within households with this assessment:

> A consideration of all forms of work suggests that, while the total amount of work done is more likely to be increasing rather than declining for most

households, new divisions of labour are emerging. It seems clear that the distribution of all forms of work is becoming increasingly unbalanced. A process of polarization is developing, with households busily engaged in all forms of work at one pole and households unable to do a wide range of work at the other.[1]

This affirmation from detailed empirical evidence that there is a close connection between employment, pay and other types of work and activity which contribute to human wellbeing is important because it sets in its proper context the discussion about alternatives based on experiences in the informal economy.

The informal economy is not a substitute for the formal economy; it exists alongside it in a relationship of dependency or symbiosis. The time is ripe for a full and realistic assessment of informal economic activity, which until recently has been under-reported and undervalued. There is a "household" model, which appears to ensure that what is produced, how it is produced and for whom it is produced, are decided in a democratic manner which is appropriate to household and community needs. However, it would be naive to assume that this model can be easily adapted to another scale. What does seem certain is that as unemployment continues on the present scale, as conventional economic policies continue to fail, and as conservative governments promote values of individualism and self-reliance, informal activity will assume greater importance and visibility and there will be a premium on informal entrepreneurial skills.

This changing reality presents a profound challenge to certain deep-seated attitudes to work, whether paid or unpaid, whether done for an employer or oneself. It is widely recognized that these attitudes have their origins in the industrial revolution and are closely bound up with religious beliefs. The phrase "Protestant work ethic" has passed from Max Weber's historical sociology into general currency. However, the debate about the "work ethic" is possibly even more confused than the discussion of labour market trends where there is a better empirical basis for generalization.

The problem of the work ethic is not a simple one because it relates to three distinct aspects of contemporary culture. First, there is what might more appropriately be described as the ideology of work. This is the expression of basic values about the meaning and worth of work (usually seen as being synonymous with employment) in the dominant institutions of industry and the state. In its managerial form it is an ethic of performance and achievement such that a person's employment in a particular position defines who and what they are in society. It is of course closely related to economic theories which tend to concentrate on the formal economy to the neglect of informal activity which equally deserves to be called "work".

The second point of reference in discussion about the work ethic is the attitudes which ordinary people bring to their work and employment. Here it is more widely recognized that people have complex motivations for working which obviously include basic survival and subsistence but extend to the desire for self-betterment in both material and non-material ways. The belief that work is done for personal fulfilment and not simply for pay is often taken to be evidence of a strong work ethic. Those who regard unemployment in an instrumental way and see it as an unpleasant necessity are said to have a weak work ethic. There is a clear possibility here that the discussion about the work ethic will proceed at cross-purposes because the prevailing ideology of work is happy to regard work (i.e. employment) in narrow, economistic terms as an activity done for material reward. Those concerned with human values in actual working life, on the other hand, are more concerned to extend the definition of the work ethic to embrace productive activity in all spheres regardless of remuneration. Indeed, some would argue that the term "work ethic" should be replaced by "life ethic" to make the point clear.

The third element in the discussion of values and the future of work is prescriptive. There are some working in the field of ethics, including those from religious backgrounds, who are attempting to set out a normative framework for the evaluation of work in its present and future forms. The present time is significant because the prospects for dialogue between these different perspectives on work are particularly good. The uncertainty about employment trends, the sense that new patterns of working are emerging in the informal sector and, more importantly, the sensed need for a coherent value framework for policy-making, all work in this direction. One of the reasons why this debate has not really taken off is that the ethical questions are not seriously addressed by those with the power to make socially significant decisions. To let the market decide is to abdicate responsibility for matters which do lie within the sphere of political decision and which are open to general understanding and judgment. The churches and other sections of society (including education and the media) have an important role to play in keeping these questions on the political agenda.

This is one of the objectives of this publication. It is organized in three parts which reflect the three questions considered by the participants at the Glasgow conference. These are followed by a conclusion based on the reports and recommendations of sub-groups. The first question and the first part of the book have to do with the assumptions behind present policies towards new technologies and employment. The contributions in this section provide some of the background information and the kind of expert reflection on current trends which enable the reader to see things in a broader perspective than is usually supplied either by official sources or the media. They also provide points of reference for those who are struggling for a footing alongside the victims of these times of change. Theodor Leuenberger sets the scene by portraying the current crisis as part of an extended period of "turbulence" in western industrial societies, as they move towards the "information society". He is quite clear that there is no hope of a return to full employment for the foreseeable, planable future and that policies must reflect this. This begs the question of how far this whole process of industrial restructuring is amenable to social and political control. The question is partly answered in a review of policies in three countries showing that there is genuine room for manoeuvre and that this might well be increased by a greater degree of international cooperation and coordination of policies. Leuenberger's conclusion is that our approach to the future must involve an attitude of flexibility and readiness to accept change, combined with the imagination to develop alternative types of economic activity—a theme which finds strong echoes in David Simpson's contribution.

All too often, technology is made the idol or the scapegoat in the story which is unfolding. Bruce Williams issues a reminder that the problem of technology is far from new and that technical change can affect employment in several different ways, the net effect of which is not necessarily to increase or diminish employment levels. Within the market system, he says, there is no mechanism to ensure that the labour-creating and labour-displacing effects of technical change are always kept in balance. Reflecting on our present predicament, he considers the relationships between productivity, hours worked and pay, and cautions against the simplistic assumption that a reduction in average hours worked in order to share the available work would provide a satisfactory solution to unemployment. In contrast to Leuenberger, and arguing from historical evidence (it is interesting to note that all three authors in the first section refer to the theory of economic development in the work of Joseph Schumpeter) he questions the view that labour-saving technical change will become more and more dominant and that "full employment" is a thing of the past. David Simpson examines in further detail the particular form and characteristics of the post-war "mixed economy" and speculates on its future. Like Leuenberger, he considers that economic activity is likely to become highly decentralized, and suggests that this will have benefits for family and community life.

The perspective of these early chapters ranges from the historical past of the industrial countries to their long-term future. The reader who is totally immersed in the here-and-now of policy-making or simply coping with the day-to-day realities of employment restructuring and job dislocation could be excused for passing them over as too far removed from the real world of action and commitment. However, it is our conviction that practical policies will be better for being informed by such discussions and should avoid foreclosing on options (full employment, reduced employment, restructured employment) which should be kept open.

The second part of the book on current employment policies and assumptions presents a series of views from practitioners in management, trade unions, state and international agencies. These shorter chapters reflect the range of perspectives which exist in the European context and the differences and similarities between them. They provide an interesting contrast to the previous section. For the most part, their outlook is focused on the shorter term, the immediate priorities and the grounds for hope and action in the present situation. What they have in common is a profound concern about the present methods of managing technological and social change and a determination to act rather than acquiesce in its effects. The reader is invited to examine what is said in the light of the earlier chapters and to consider whether industry is taking up the role of free agent which conservative governments are anxious to give it, whether special measures for youth training or job creation are mere "placebo" responses, and so on. If, as many suspect, the institutions of private enterprise, the large trade unions and the state are involved essentially in crisis management, no amount of sophistication or fine-tuning will bring us closer to the longer-term goals which must be defined.

The present work ethic and prospects for an alternative are the themes of Part III. David Bleakley's contribution is a powerful plea for a new and truer measurement of the value of work—one that will take us beyond equating work only with a paid job supplied through the market. He gives expression to the sense of transition which many workers are feeling and the growing consensus in political and trade union circles that policies must be directed towards alternatives which break down the distinction between employment and unemployment, work and non-work. There are, of course, formidable obstacles to doing this, both in the nature of the market system and in the current priorities of workers and unions. In a chapter on work ideologies and prospects for participation Peter Cressey shows how the economic recession has actually led to reduced worker participation, and made it more difficult at the enterprise level to examine the alternatives which most policy makers agree in principle should be explored.

If David Bleakley is concerned with broad theological and ideological questions, and Peter Cressey is concerned with the conditions affecting workers' attitudes to work and participation, Göran Collste explores the third aspect of work ethics, namely the kind of normative framework or theory which could be used to evaluate technological change and employment policies. Such a project is highly ambitious and raises fundamental questions about theological and ethical approaches and the role of the churches in promoting certain values which others in society may or may not share. The chapter presents the outline of an approach which has rarely entered into discussions of the work ethic. It is on a par with earlier attempts to define the "right to work" as a basic human right but instead departs from an understanding of human needs which work should be organized to fulfill.

The final section of the book sets out the edited reports and recommendations of the sub-groups at the Glasgow workshop. In the spirit of ecumenical enquiry and commitment to people in their situation of need, they are addressed primarily to the churches, but in the belief that an informed and practical response by them will necessarily involve close cooperation with other agencies and individuals who share the same concern to find alternatives to the meaningless, empty and dependent life-styles which many in and out of employment experience, and to counter the fear which change typically creates.

Our exploration needs to be set within the context of previous ecumenical social thinking. The 1983 Vancouver Assembly of the World Council of Churches replaced the "Just, Participatory and Sustainable Society" (JPSS) by commitment to covenant for "Justice, Peace and the Integrity of Creation" (JPIC). The change may have occurred because the concept of sustainability, originally intended to relate justice to the whole of creation, was suspect on account of its presumed association with the "limits to growth" thinking of the Club of Rome. Specific reference to peace, now recognized as inseparable from justice, reflects the concerns of peace movements both within and outside the churches, while participation continues to be implicit.

Be this as it may, the integrity of creation stands for much that was encapsulated by sustainability. It is less anthropocentric, and arguably more biblical. To say, as some have done, that sustainability is inappropriate because it appears nowhere in the Old and New Testaments, is to belie the whole "middle axioms" approach of ecumenical social ethics from the responsible (or just) society onwards. It is precisely because the Bible does not address certain specific contemporary social issues that notions such as JPSS and JPIC must be elaborated.

The integrity of creation stands for our long-term global commitment to justice, peace and the wellbeing of the entire ecosystem. More than any other "middle axiom" it stresses the links between the three elements, and suggests a basis for ethically appropriate action (a person of integrity, for example, is someone who is not only descriptively integrated, but also acts accordingly). Thus, whatever the wisdom or otherwise of jettisoning sustainability, the new phrase can be interpreted to include much that the earlier term stood for, i.e. environmental responsibility, resource sharing, the interdependency of humanity, nature and God.

Work is primarily a "justice" issue, though there are many places in the following chapters where it is clearly inseparable from peace (i.e. relationships within a healthy society) and ecology concerns. But the three contributions dealing with work ethics, though people- rather than systems-orientated, do not primarily address major biblical and theological issues, and it is here that future research will have to be carried out.

The last major WCC contribution to the theological understanding of work was Alan Richardson's *The Biblical Doctrine of Work*, published in 1952.[2] This was a response by biblical scholars to J.H. Oldham's *Work in Modern Society*, published two years earlier, and was taken up under the heading "The Christian in his Vocation" at the WCC's Second Assembly at Evanston in 1954.[3] Neither of these two authors could have anticipated in the early fifties the extent to which structural unemployment would have become endemic by the 1980s. It is not surprising, therefore, that some of their assumptions are no longer valid. There is, however, one major theological affirmation by Alan Richardson which currently assumes an even greater importance than when it was first written, and it concerns the eucharistic significance of work. From the fifth century onwards, the word "liturgy" has been used primarily to denote the church's main act of worship, the eucharist. The notion of the eucharistic offering whereby the people offer to God their oblations, though temporarily obscured by the mediaeval doctrine of sacrifice, reasserted itself in Anglicanism and elsewhere (though not in the Lutheran church).

As members of Christ's body, Christians celebrating their regular eucharist offer to God themselves, their souls and bodies (Rom. 12:1). Thus in this aspect the church's eucharist is an offering of the body of Christ from within which context the people present the labour of their hands—the bread and wine which are laid upon the altar.

Richardson points out that this aspect of the eucharist and its relevance to the biblical doctrine of work was seldom emphasized prior to the present century, but that recognition of it has brought a new dimension of reality into the worship of many a working-class congregation (it has also been incorporated into the WCC's Lima Liturgy). Tragically, it is precisely those congregations which seem to have been most renewed by such theological rediscoveries in their worship which are currently most hard hit by mass unemployment. It is therefore perhaps not inappropriate to hope that the implementation of some of the practical measures recommended to churches in the closing section of this book—especially with regard to the need for a redefinition or replacement of the Protestant work ethic – will go hand in hand with a rediscovery of the relationship between work and worship.

NOTES

1. *Divisions of Labour*, Oxford, Basil Blackwell, 1984.
2. London, SCM Press, 1963.
3. London, SCM Press, 1950.

PART I

Technology and the Future of Work

Global Trends in Employment: Problems and Strategies

THEODOR LEUENBERGER

Few people would disagree that the next 10 to 20 years will bring great turbulence to our societies, whatever their stage of development. How we deal with this period will be of crucial importance for our long-term future. "Turbulence" describes the unpredictable and unmanageable situations which we are now experiencing. Our task, as I understand it, is to work out a common frame of reference and to study ways of dealing with the different aspects of social dislocation and conflict. "Politics", Max Weber once remarked, "is the strenuous slow drilling of hard boards. It takes both passion and perspective." These qualities are essential if we are to work out a shared view of the nature of the problems and appropriate policies for dealing with them.

In the turbulence of the transition to what is often called the information society, existing gaps between countries and groups and individuals will increase. The information society develops new kinds of "haves" and "have-nots" with respect to the creation of information, access to it and the ability to use it effectively. A century ago about 10 per cent of the labour force were involved in information working, now about 30 per cent. This signifies a process of rapid growth in the information structure in our societies and a change in the knowledge structure, the rapid "informatization" of society.

The terms "high technology", "knowledge-based", "information-based" are interchangeable in descriptions of the new information economy in which the strategic resource is information rather than the classic machine technology. Present modern and modernizing societies are driven by the growth of information as the dominant resource. The changing structure of occupations reflects this process. Information occupations are defined as positions in which the creation, processing and distribution of information are performed:
— information producers create new information;
— information processors receive and respond to information inputs (administrative staff);
— information distributors convey information to the recipient;

— information infrastructure personnel carry out maintenance work.[1]
All these occupations are increasing in size and importance.

Information as the dominant resource is very different from what have hitherto been called our scarce *resources*. Unlike raw materials, land or labour, information is not depletive. It is expandable and actually grows with use. Of course, the accumulation of knowledge has always been a characteristic of our development, but continued accumulation leads to an acceleration of the rate of development as a whole. So this permanent accumulation of new scientific-technical knowledge has a revolutionary quality. Technical and economic changes are taking place so fast that social change cannot cope any more. The tasks of information processing extend far beyond the skills of the traditional working population. One result of this is the rapid deskilling of critical occupations and age-groups. It is of the greatest importance and urgency, therefore, to understand the relationships between *technology, work and employment*.

There is increasing interdependence between present technological developments and economic and social structures, and within this the relationship between technology, productivity growth and employment is crucial. Since the high growth rate period of the 1960s, there have been tremendous productivity gains. The problem is that with ever-increasing productivity growth, unemployment must grow unless there is parallel drop in working hours or a slowing down of the productivity gains. But we cannot artificially protect declining sectors. This is the competitivity-productivity paradox. It requires that we accept unemployment today, in order to safeguard the future of employment itself. Thus the implementation of technology is a necessity, which makes unemployment worse but in the long run "less worse" than if it were not implemented. Because technological innovations will offer fewer new jobs there is no hope of a return to traditional "full employment". What J. Fourastie has called the "thirty glorious years" is over. In fact, the whole social democratic programme based on the macro-economic management of a mixed economy and the extension of the welfare state is called in question. What, then, has to be done?

Cultural change and technological change

The quantitative impact of technology on employment is only the tip of the iceberg. The underlying problem is the qualitative and structural change in existing jobs. This is the object of a major programme in the European Community (FAST) which is attempting to assess possible future developments through the following areas of study:
— the construction of European scenarios for work;
— the future of certain categories of workers and employees with a view to highlighting the critical occupations;

— study of the transformation of industrial sectors starting from the scientific and technological innovations in progress between now and the year 2000.[2]

With regard to work scenarios, a number of questions emerge. What are the new working patterns? Will we see common patterns in all societies, apart from the factors which are specific to local and national conditions? One salient feature of the transformation of work in all western societies is the transition from the standard "block" working pattern to a more "open" pattern. What will be the direction and rhythm of the transformation? Where are the opportunities, where are the major risks? Typical career patterns are certain to be altered. There are careers in the ascendant (brain-workers) and in decline (manual workers).

New categories of brain-workers are developing: for the design and operation of flexible workshops and expert systems; for communications via the electronic networks which will develop in the 1990s; and for the applications on which the new information technologies and the new bio-technologies converge.

One problem specific to Europe is the aging of our populations. The growing number of workers and employees aged 50 and over poses problems. We will see an active population no longer containing a majority of young adults but rather of mature adults with a clustering of the active population in their fifties. The aging of the population in Europe has consequences for work. Towards the year 2000 between 15 and 20 per cent of the population will be over 65. If these men and women are sent into early retirement at 55 or 60 to make room for younger people we are likely to see the further development of alternative forms of work, including semi-active, voluntary, clandestine and "black" working.[3]

In short we need to prepare for a social structure in which only part of the working population will be needed to produce all the goods and services (i.e. an extension to the industry economy of a phenomenon which already exists in agriculture). We must do away with the single, salaried and full-time job syndrome and promote a pluralistic society based on plural activities for its members. It will require a vast training and redeployment programme to respond to the new skill requirements. It will amount to a transformation of the function of education and training itself.

Education and training patterns will play a decisive part in the response of our societies to the "third industrial revolution" and there is already much reflection on educational restructuring. One proposal is that it should consist of a global package incorporating educational policies, labour market policies and social policies. Clearly there has to be a change away from the traditional sequence: schooling, working years, years of retirement.

One suggestion is to introduce a system of recurrent education in which it would be possible to combine or alternate periods of education, work and retirement throughout adult life. The immediate priority should be a second cycle of re-education for those aged 40–50 and the expansion of an open system of continuing education.

At present, socio-cultural realities are not evolving in parallel to the techno-economic changes. Culturally speaking, we have failed to come to grips with the phenomena of rapid technological change.

Models of development

Still significant in an evolutionary perspective are Schumpeter's innovation theory and Gerhard Mensch's theory of waves of basic innovations. For Schumpeter, technical innovation was the mainspring of capitalist development. In fact, an economic evolutionary process consists of the trinity of invention, innovation and diffusion of innovations.[4] Schumpeter proposed that "technical innovations proceed by jerks and rushes".[5] Technological change is not a smooth incremental and continuous process. Innovations are more like a series of explosions than a gentle transformation. From such a perspective, economic growth in any economy, developed or less developed, must be viewed as a *disequilibrium process*.[6] The key development process Schumpeter identified as the "carrying out of new combinations" and "new combinations mean the competitive elimination of the old". There are winners and losers. The bunching of basic innovations has a bandwagon effect—it explains the upswings in the long waves and the elimination of old products and processes. The innovation phase can be described as the rolling of several new technology band wagons—the computer band wagon, the bio-technology band wagon etc. It is the speed, scope and complexity of this phase which sets the information economy apart from the "smokestack" industries. The push of innovation demands new skills and employment practices, a more flexible research environment, higher labour mobility, and new industrial structures.

The path of social development in the innovation phase must include appropriate measures, both public and private, for risk reduction and risk diffusion. This is one of the most striking features of Japan's relatively successful political economy. Structures for risk taking and risk reduction will be decisive in the present transition period. We neglect them at our peril and in the certainty of doing great harm to vulnerable groups in society, including youth, women, older workers and ethnic minorities. However, social policy and labour market policy on their own are incomplete. It needs to be part of a more global package, which includes innovation policy, technology policy, economic policy and industrial policy. With such a policy package we have to prepare a new approach to manufacturing production based on electronics and information technology. At the centre of the present debate about manufacturing is the concept of the flexible manufacturing system (FMS). The current term used in French is *ateliers flexibles* (flexible workshops). The concept of "integrated flexible systems" implies a radical revolution relative to pre-FMS industry. They integrate instead of subdivide the manufacturing process and they are flexible, instead of locking the industrial process into a fixed sequence. New materials (steel, more and more plastic metals, a new generation of ceramics) and the new "technologies of light" (lasers, fibre optics, systems for the capture, processing, exploitation of image data) present another challenge to the flexibility and adaptability of industry. All these technologies and materials are in their infancy. We will have to evaluate the creative potential which the new technologies, the new materials, the new flexible systems represent. This must include an assessment of their impact on employment during the next 15 or 20 years. This is not only an intra-European challenge. It is global because of the international mobility of knowledge, technology and entrepreneurship.

The challenge to policy-makers is to develop policies which spread the burden of the present transitional adjustments more effectively. Such policies and strategies have to identify the target point for policy and to design strategies that can influence structures. It is clear that problems which are typically described as governmental overload, the crisis of legitimacy and simply the inability of governments to guide societal developments mean that the transformation from ad hoc crisis management to planned change cannot be achieved through government alone. What is required is a network of organizations and interorganizational cooperation. Policy-making and revising is a multi-actor game. Hence the fundamental importance of promoting understanding between the different groups involved.

Enhancing the capacity for policy innovation

Policy-making always involves organizations and institutions but institutions are slow learners. What, then, is the present policy repertoire and can we enlarge it? With regard to social policy there are two prevailing attitudes or standpoints, progressive and conservative. From a conservative point of view the present economic system is basically satisfactory but needs some social cushioning because there are negative side-effects in market economies and discontent among the less privileged groups of society must be prevented in order to preserve political stability. The progressive attitude is characterized by strong and positive engagement in social and welfare activities mainly because dynamic free-market processes are seen as a constant source of social problems, disruptions which cannot be left to the market. The techno-economic dynamics produce winners and losers and society must provide protection and compensation. Social services are not seen as a burden but as a right of citizens.

The progressive view can be equated with the "welfare state" tradition. The idea, which took root in Britain, is summed up in a pamphlet by Archbishop William Temple published in 1941,[7] where he wrote: "In place of the concept of the Power State we are led to that of the Welfare State." The idea then found practical expression in Lord Beveridge's proposals. In many countries this has been the policy response in the post-war political and social scene. However, it has been losing its base as the momentum of the post-war economic expansion has lost its force. Now few governments promote such broad long-term thinking. Public policy generally reflects a more conservative attitude and may be called a symbolic or placebo response. Some argue that the unemployment problem demands placebo policies because it is so difficult to solve in reality. The sheer scale of the problem (in terms of numbers of people unemployed), its inter-relationship with other policy areas, and the complex interdependency of international economic relations all limit national options. Roger Henning and Jeremy Richardson write: "Unemployment may be a singularly intractable problem forcing governments to engage in manipulative and symbolic activity in order to reduce the political costs of failure."[8] Or: "'Successful' responses are those that transfer the political costs from the government of the day to other actors in the political process."[9]

The question is whether the fundamental restructuring process is beyond our political capacity to control. As the restructuring of the world's economies proceeds almost regardless, can governments do much more than apply clean bandages to the inevitable wounds?

Managing unemployment

Policy-makers have in practice to make a response in concrete policy terms. Let us now review the range of policy choices selected by governments in the USA, France and the Federal Republic of Germany. For all of them the key problem is the mismatch between skills or skill-levels and job requirements. Thus the adjustment and redeployment of human capital is the focal topic. While there are economic and technical aspects to this, of greatest interest to us here is the political management of the unemployment problem.

USA

Beginning with the 1946 Employment Act the role of the government in employment and training was clearly expressed. In the 1960s, employment and training programmes expanded as strategies in the war on poverty. Federal job creation projects were developed. In 1971 the

Emergency Employment Act authorized a two-year Public Employment Programme. This was the largest public job creation programme since the Great Depression and was very broadly targeted. To be eligible participants had to have been unemployed only one week. Targeted groups included Vietnam veterans, youth, older workers, migrants, non-English-speaking workers, welfare recipients, disadvantaged persons, even displaced scientists. In retrospect, it is possible to see that the programme was implemented too quickly and decelerated too abruptly to provide definite answers and solutions. The public employment programmes shared a common philosophy that workers who are unemployed, not for want of skill but because of a recession or depression, are entitled to maintain a minimum standard of living through government sponsored jobs so long as unsubsidized employment remains unavailable to them. Programmes of this kind are attractive because they combine maintenance of job skills with income transfer that lacks the social stigma of welfare payments. For young people such a work experience combined with training gives a better understanding of work-place standards, greater knowledge about occupations. For older workers, the chance to work on a socially useful project provides needed income and increased self-esteem.

The assumption behind most public job creation programmes is that they will be needed until the individual can move into the normal labour market. Unfortunately, however, for many there is no realistic expectation in this direction. Government has for them the role of the employer of last resort.

Such a programme which assigns to the government the role of employer of last resort may not be feasible on a national scale. Another measure used is skill training. It helps to make persons more employable by increasing their knowledge and skills. The 1962 Manpower Development and Training Act, for example, is an instrument for federally subsidized skill training on the job or in institutional training. In addition there are apprenticeship training periods from one to six years.

There is some concern that this kind of assistance limits opportunities for persons who are not selected for training and that certain programme admission standards may screen out minorities and women. For example, fewer than one in five apprentices were members of minority groups in 1980, while only 6 per cent were women.[10]

Improving skills is one type of assistance. Another is job search assistance, which includes many activities like vocational counselling, aptitude testing, information on the labour market, relocation of workers etc. But the Job Service received criticism from its clients, both job seekers and employers. The job seekers claimed that the Job Service was not responsive to their actual needs and had become "employer-oriented". At the same time many employers deserted the system because in their view the Job Service was concentrating its efforts on the placement of the poor and disadvantaged rather than meeting their business needs. In the light of these difficulties an effort was made in the 1970s to introduce performance measures into the funding process. Placements were selected as the chief measure of Job Service performance.

Adjustment assistance is a special category of employment assistance targeted to dislocated workers (e.g. in the steel or auto industries) who lose their jobs because of changing technology or foreign competition, which are beyond the workers' control. The assistance may include help with job search training, readjustment allowances and grants for relocation when another job is obtained outside the home community.

It is apparent from trends in employment and unemployment that public jobs programmes do not constitute a very effective response to structural unemployment. The most effective long-term government intervention is skill training. Training programmes seem to offer the most consistent gains. Apprenticeship that combines instruction and on-the-job training is a particularly effective approach to developing professional skills. But the small numbers of people engaged in these training programmes and the limited opportunities that were made available to women and minorities did not make it a general employment development tool.

So far the USA has no consistent, long-range approach to employment and training. This remains one of the major challenges of the 1980s. How is it likely to be met? The Reagan administration represents a profound transition in social and economic policies in the United States. In parallel with the movement away from the old industrial phase and towards a post-industrial, high technology era, in which jobs have migrated from basic industry to services and the information sector, the old Democratic New Deal coalition has been replaced by a close business-government alliance. It is a deliberate movement away from liberal social engineering with hardly any signs of a coherent social democratic alternative to prevent it. Neo-liberalism may have a chance.

A. Hirschman portrayed the alternation between "public action" and "private interest". Past experience suggests that we go through periods of action, idealism and reform; then the society becomes disenchanted with the results. We then enter a period where public action recedes and private interest dominates. For example, the twenties and forties were decades of public action. The sixties, with Johnson's Great Society and the war on poverty, represent the next season of public action. In the seventies there began another period of private interest—a period of which Reagan is the culmination. We may suppose that somewhere in the late 1980s or early 1990s the failure of the Reagan administration to solve problems will produce a significant change in the direction of public action although the signs of this have yet to emerge.

France

Employment in France has several distinctive features. There has been widespread use of immigrant labour. In the reconstruction period after 1945 a community of two million immigrant workers was created. Hiring of immigrant workers was often a substitute for investment in advanced manufacturing processes and the labour market has long been characterized by a shortage of skilled manpower. With economic stagnation, the use of immigrant labour has been called into question. This shift has been intensified by demographic changes which increased the supply of young people and women to the labour market. France also has a large public sector where security of employment is the general rule. In fact, the state is the largest employer and historically the public enterprises have always played a key role in the French economy.

After the 1978 elections Raymond Barre developed four main antiunemployment measures. The first was intended to make placement services more efficient. The second was intended to encourage workers to leave the labour market altogether. The prime target for this was immigrants, older employees and women. Immigration of foreign workers had been suspended in 1974, when there were one million registered unemployed in France and two million immigrant workers. At that time the exit of older workers from the active labour market was encouraged by an agreement which ensured that a worker leaving over the age of 60 would receive 70 per cent of his former salary. Later agreements extended this guarantee to workers under the age of 60. This costly policy of encouraging exit from the labour market became rather popular.

The third strategy of the Barre government established pacts for youth employment. The two elements of this strategy were incentives to firms that created jobs and hired young people and state aid for the preparation of young people for the labour market. Thus the idea of apprenticeship was emphasized: training contracts or practical on-the-job training were offered, with the possibility of permanent employment. However, studies showed that the "employment pacts" did not help to lessen unemployment. Many employers used the schemes to postpone permanent hiring and thus benefited from cheap temporary manpower.

The fourth strategy adopted by the Barre government was an attempt to increase flexibility in existing work contracts. On the whole the government favoured limited tenure contracts. Statistics show that during the period 1974–81 the use of temporary employment increased greatly so that temporary employment is now a widespread phenomenon.

The fate of the unemployed and the future of the economy played an important role in the presidential election campaign of 1981. The Mitterrand/Mauroy industrial policy reflected at the beginning the social policy priority given to employment. But the government faced a dilemma: on the one hand it wanted France to become a highly productive industrial society, in the vanguard of the third industrial revolution based on biotechnologies and electronics, and on the other hand it desired to maintain a diversified industrial fabric including the declining sectors.

If industry is to be capable of standing up to the most advanced competition a policy of adjustment is obviously essential. But governments tend to want everything at the same time: being internationally competitive, preserving a stable level of employment and keeping up with structural and technological change. The French government was reluctant to make certain fundamental economic choices.

The Mitterrand/Mauroy policy has been a combination of Neo-Keynesianism, technocratism and centralized socialism. With regard to employment policy there is a strong interest in professional training programmes and a separate ministry exists for this purpose. The new ministry works on both short- and long-term strategies. The budget for professional training was increased by 28 per cent. The idea of training for a new job while keeping the old job was reaffirmed. In addition there are the "Rigout" programmes which combine theoretical training periods and practical professional training periods. Encouragement is given to employers who hire young people by exempting them from welfare insurance payments etc. Finally, the idea of removing older workers from the labour market is continued. "Solidarity contracts" have been promoted which allow early retirement from the age of 55 and permit young people to be hired for these vacant positions.

It was proposed that new jobs be created by "work sharing" and reductions in working hours. The theme of work sharing had been developed earlier, particularly by Jacques Delors. The Mauroy government expressed the goal in terms of an average of 35 hours of work per week by 1985. On 16 January 1982 Ordinance lowered the legal working hours to 39 hours without specifying that the salary levels should be maintained. The result was that employers reduced salaries by 2.5 per cent. Later Pierre Mauroy was to concede that more jobs for more people with fewer hours correspond to less money earned.[11]

The Mitterrand/Mauroy employment policies consisted of a combination of innovation and continuity. In the meantime the Socialists found that unemployment cannot be fought in isolation from other economic problems and from other national economies. The interdependence of the world's economies means that macro-economic policies have to be coordinated. Transnational tendencies and structures determine and limit national policy choices. For example, there exists a Project Link analysis which showed how West Germany, Japan, the United States and United Kingdom could jointly engineer an economic recovery.[12] So far, however, advocacy of better coordination has been stronger than actual implementation. The 1978 Bonn summit was the first example of a macro-economic policy package adopted by the major economies.

The lesson of the Mitterrand policy is that unilateral (expansionary) policies are difficult to sustain and very costly. In my view *all* countries in the OECD can benefit in terms of their own policy goals from a coordinated package of macro-economic policies.

Federal Republic of Germany

In the 1950s and 1960s the Federal Republic of Germany presented one of the most successful models of economic development in the post-war period. It had all the elements of economic and social stability:
— an active stabilization and growth policy employing new instruments for macro-economic management;
— the inclusion of labour unions together with employers associations and business organizations in corporatist political management;
— an active social welfare policy providing a minimum income guarantee to everybody.

This social economic policy package afforded German society protection against the risk of political unrest which might grow out of mass unemployment. Organized labour, in fact, made an essential contribution to the post-war period of political stability and economic growth. Collective bargaining and corporatist arrangements (*Sozialpartnerschaft*) were important stabilizing mechanisms and the unions became reliable partners of government. Of course as highly centralized powerful union organizations they are in a better position to influence and control rank-and-file behaviour than craft or occupationally-based unions.

The Federal Republic of Germany, like other western European countries, suffered large job losses with the onset of the economic crisis in the 1970s but it was several years before there was an attempt by the social-liberal coalition to pursue an aggressive anti-unemployment policy. This was the investment programme which ran from 1978 to 1980. The main elements of this programme included public investment in the transport system, environmental protection and improvement and energy conservation. The programme was supported by an expansionary budgetary policy.

The employment effects were positive. Half of the 900,000 increase in wage- and salary-earners' jobs between 1978 and 1980 could be attributed to the expansionary orientation of budgetary policy. But on the whole labour market policy, personnel policies and special programmes to boost employment were all subordinated to a restrictive budgetary policy.

This trend was indicative of a widespread philosophy of economic management. It was dominant in the end phase of the social-liberal coalition: the direct vote of the government in creating and protecting employment was limited and the job of fighting unemployment was left to market forces. Over the period 1974 to 1984 the bias of employment policy and the scale of federal government intervention to influence economic development changed several times according to the general budgetary policy steered by the coalition. The scale of intervention rose in 1975, contracted in 1976–77, expanded again between 1978 and 1980 and was then reduced in 1981–82. Overall, the trend was towards a reduction of direct intervention in the labour market. This was true for personnel policy, public investment, employment subsidies and job creation schemes. At the beginning of the 1980s we enter a period where public action recedes and private interest dominates. We see the same dominance of trickle-down economics, or supply-side economics, the crusade against regulation, the desire to reduce the government apparatus which emerged during the latter years of coalition government.

The case of the Federal Republic of Germany between 1975 and 1982 indicates that unemployment levels can be lowered by deliberate public action (active government employment policies) and increased by inactive policies. To this extent, at least, policy can influence structures. High levels of unemployment persisted in 1976 and 1977 when government policy was passive. Later, from 1978–80, with a more active anti-unemployment policy, some reduction was achieved despite an expanding labour force. The abandonment of this policy coincided with a steep rise in unemployment. Throughout all this it became apparent that the German political system, like others in western Europe, can absorb quite high levels of unemployment without severe social conflict and political instability, provided basic needs in housing, health care, food and education are being met.

The challenge of changing structures

The most obvious conclusion to any review of current policies in these or any other countries in the Organization for Economic Cooperation and Development (OECD) is that full-employment policies or even policies oriented towards full-employment in the longer term are essentially rhetorical. The general retreat from such a policy has been a response to economic constraints and a changing philosophy of economic crisis management. With the British example as an extreme case, the general preference is for neo-liberal crisis management policy. Full employment is abandoned as a goal of economic policy because there is no need for it or any kind of social policy in a real growth economy. According to Blum we need less protection and more work opportunities; in Reagan's terms, workfare not welfare.

The point of substance here is that western Europe is made up of old, stable societies in a network of rigid bureaucratic institutions which are in part responsible for the economic decline.[13] Stable societies tend to stagnation, to more and more regulation and their innovative capacity is reduced. This is the kernel of truth in the rhetoric of Reagonomics, and Thatcherism. The crucial factor responsible for the decline and unemployment is inflexibility and ossified structures.

What would be the consequences of demanding greater flexibility in structures of employment/work? Part-time working, for example, accounts for one third of all new jobs in the USA. Elsewhere, there are signs of a new distribution between paid and unpaid work, new jobs and activities where people can determine their own conditions, a different distribution of work, reducing or varying its length and ensuring a suitable minimum income for all, including people outside the labour force. The present system of employment operates like a force pump. So far the dynamics of societies are still focused on work, production, economy, efficiency and rationality. Such work-centred models will be inadequate in future and more life-centred structures and perspectives will have to be developed. There is a question-mark over industrial employment as the centrepoint for our social and personal identity.

With massive unemployment as a norm, a growing part of the population needs other focal points. In a "culture of unemployment" (Gorz) we see developing subcultures of an informal economy. Here the centrality of work orientation and productivity is gone. The industrial concepts of work and worth no longer grip. Self-help groups in the interstices of the old system have a new framework beyond the employment and production sphere. The boundaries become fluid between employment, unemployment and inactivity. New patterns of activity are developing outside industry and outside the traditional public sector. They arise in small-scale social and commercial services, in a wide range of small-scale production and artistic work as well as in voluntary networks. They include a wide variety of high-quality artistic and cultural services, more diversified and responsive health services, individual and group counselling and a variety of active leisure-time interests.

These are the areas where demand is likely to grow in the future. What is needed are new organizational and financial arrangements which help the matching of demand and supply in these emerging fields of quality services and consumption. There are models of such arrangements namely the remainders of the cooperative movements. I doubt that big business, big unions and big state bureaucracies with their traditional strategies and instruments can help much to facilitate these new employment opportunities. The best they can do is to allow the development of a wide variety of small scale, decentralized, differentiated, commercial, cooperative and voluntary organizations matching the needs of a population which is no longer dominated by the traditional forms of employment in the private and public sectors.

To conclude: the dominant coalition of big business, big unions and big government which has successfully managed modern post-war capitalism is now confronted with many new and severe challenges. Some of these can be met by government and business. But the challenges of technological unemployment and changes in motivation will not be met with adequate responses because the centralized, corporatist solutions of recent decades will be more of a hindrance than a help to finding new and flexible patterns and structures.

NOTES

1. Ref. OECD *Information Activities, Electronics and Telecommunications Technologies*, ICCP 6, Vol. 1, 1981.
2. FAST 1984-87, Objectives and Work Programme, EEC Brussels, p.25.
3. *Ibid.*, p.27.
4. R.R. Nelson and S. Winter, *An Evolutionary Theory of Economic Change*, Harvard, 1982; E. Rogers ed., *The Diffusion of Innovations*, 3rd ed., Free Press, 1983.
5. J.A. Schumpeter, *Capitalism, Socialism and Democracy*, London, 1949.
6. Nelson and Winter, *op. cit.*, p.236.
7. *Citizen and Churchman*, 1941.
8. *Unemployment, Policy Responses of Western Democracies*, Sage, 1984, p.5.
9. *Ibid.*, p.25.
10. US Department of Labour Employment and Training, Report of the President, 1981.
11. *Le Monde*, 12 February 1982.
12. Michael Stewart, *The Age of Interdependence: Economic Policy in a Shrinking World*, MIT Press, 1984.
13. M. Olson, *The Rise and Decline of Nations*, New Haven, 1982.

Chips and Robots

BRUCE WILLIAMS

Technical change is not a modern invention. The distinction between the stone age, bronze age and iron age is technical; museums in China provide ample evidence of a great range of inventions and innovations in ancient China. The adoption of gunpowder in the fourteenth century transformed warfare and, like the invention of movable type and type metal in the fifteenth century, was a technical change with profound social and economic consequences. But increasingly from the second half of the eighteenth century technical change took on a new significance—it became more self-sustaining, pervasive and cumulative in nature.

Advances in scientific knowledge and inventions do not of themselves change methods of production. Many new discoveries and inventions with potentially great practical significance have remained unused for generations. They may remain unused from lack of capital to invest in them, or from the lack of a technical capacity to make them work well. Watt's first steam engines, for example, were very inefficient because machine shops could not work to the tolerances required for efficiency. In the 1920s Taylor and Woollard invented an automatic transfer machine which failed in its application to the production of engines at Britain's Coventry plant of Morris Motors because the electric, hydraulic and pneumatic control equipment of that time was not sufficiently reliable. Fifty years later advances in electronics and in particular in microprocessors made possible the effective use of much more complex automatic devices than the Taylor-Woollard transfer machine. Highly automated and flexible manufacturing systems are now possible today.

In his *Wealth of Nations* (1776) Adam Smith foreshadowed a process of cumulative change by treating labour-saving inventions as a consequence of the division of labour, and division of labour as a consequence of the size of markets. As workers came to specialize in particular operations, they would invent methods of saving their labour; as making machinery became a specialized operation, the manufacturers would invent better machines; and then as science became a specialized occupation, the invention process would become more general.

Eighty years later in his work, *Grundrisse*, Marx observed the effects of greater specialization and capital accumulation on productivity, and wrote that in advanced capitalism, all the sciences were pressed into the service of capital and invention was made a part of business. Still later, in *Capitalism, Socialism and Democracy*, published in 1942, Schumpeter claimed that large corporations were now able to use their research, design and development departments to make process and product innovations "to order", consequently making innovation a routine business function.

In *Science and Society*, A.N. Whitehead wrote that "the greatest invention of the nineteenth century was the invention of the art of invention". Likewise, the "planned invention" of the atom bomb during the war, "the planned invention" of nuclear power stations after the war, the confident decision to put a man on the moon and bring him back again, and the high rates of industrial innovation in, for example, aircraft, synthetics, electronics and food technology, appeared for a time to justify Schumpeter's generalization.

However the productivity downturn from the mid-sixties, and the signs that once again there had been a bunching of the innovation process, made it clear that if large corporations are capable of turning out innovations to order, the research scientists and engineers need time to do so, and that either not enough of the next generation of innovations were ordered from them at the proper times, or it is not clear what that next generation should be. Innovation is still pervasive and cumulative, but it is not a smooth and continuous process, for it has important disruptive as well as constructive growth effects.

Consequences

The successful production of new technologies to reduce costs of production or improve the qualities of established products or to launch new products has resulted in very large increases in the production of goods and services per capita of population in the industrialized countries. Between 1820 and 1980, product per head increased by factors of between 13 to 18 in France, Federal Republic of Germany, Japan, Sweden, Switzerland and the USA. The increase was less in the United Kingdom and the Netherlands, though had their levels of product per capita been as low as those in Germany and Sweden in 1820, they too would have shown increases of over 13.

This growth in material wealth made possible increases in formal education, in research, in leisure, in housing, in sanitation and in health. The increase in life expectancy was the result of a reduction in dangerous, back-breaking occupations, better public health measures, increases in medical knowledge and vaccines, and greater and more certain food supplies. One of the most important consequences of industrialization has been the increase in the capacity to produce, transport and store food. World population is now at least seven times greater than two hundred years ago when Malthus wrote to warn that wars, famine and disease would check the growth of population unless growth was kept under control by "moral restraints". During the rapid growth of population in the last fifty years, the growth in the output of food has been kept slightly ahead, though of course not in all regions. Demographers predict a further doubling of world population in the next hundred years unless the Malthusian restraints become powerful, but the signs are that it will be possible to increase food supplies by at least one or two factors. Recent developments in the biological sciences, and in bio-technologies such as genetic engineering give promise of further increases in the production of food.

That growth in population created problems of pollution, with a doubling of population creating further problems, is not as serious as the effect of technical change on war technology. That has now reached a state which poses a serious threat to continued human life on earth. Other costs of technical changes have brought about pollution due to the discharge of wastes into rivers and the burning of fossil fuels, rural depopulation, the creation of depressed areas, and the decline in demand for many hard-earned human skills and the recurrence of periods of heavy unemployment.

There was unemployment before the industrial revolution which started in the second half of the eighteenth century, but it was episodic not regular, being caused by wars and the vagaries of nature. It seems that in the last hundred and fifty years, average unemployment has been higher than in earlier times. But although technical change seems to have increased the incidence of unemployment, and although during periods of depressions in industrial societies there are always fears for the future of employment, there has not been a tendency for a trend increase in unemployment. The depressions of the 1870s and 1930s, for example, were followed by periods of substantial growth in employment, and then during the 1960s and 1970s full or near full employment was sustained for an unusually long period of time.

Technological unemployment?

Although fears for the future of employment are not new, today's literature on "chips and robots" has generated more and stronger fears for the future of employment than ever before. In *Work in Crisis* the Rev. Roger Clarke gave clear expression to a widespread suspicion that "the inherited work ethic, with its adulation of the worker and the moral condemnation of those who do not work, is becoming increasingly anachronistic and unhelpful in an age where jobs have become a scarce resource". Such judgments, made so soon after an unusually long period of full employment, either imply a sharp shift in the balance between the labour-displacing and the labour-extending nature of technical change, or ignorance of past recoveries from depressions in employment.

Technical change affects unemployment in three primary ways:
1. Process innovations that reduce labour cause unemployment when the percentage increase in output which follows is less than the percentage reduction of labour per unit output.
2. Process innovations that reduce labour per unit output actually increase employment when, in response to reductions in price, the percentage increase in output is greater than the percentage reduction of labour per unit output.
3. Product innovations which create new markets extend the demand for labour.

Process innovations in agriculture have increased output per acre and reduced labour per unit output. But the capacity of the human stomach is limited, and the percentage increase in real output has been less than the percentage reductions in the labour required for each unit of real output, whether a bushel of wheat or a bale of wool. The application of science to agriculture has led to a reduction in the proportion of the work force in agriculture, even in countries such as the USA, Canada, and Australia which are substantial exporters of food. Since 1870, in Britain the percentage of the labour force has fallen from 23 to 2.5, in Australia from 30 to 6, in the USA from 50 to 3.5, in Germany from 50 to 6, in France from 50 to 8, and in Japan and Finland from over 70 to 11. Technical change in agriculture has displaced labour from agriculture on a very large scale.

If there had not been such a displacement of labour from agriculture, the opportunity to increase the real output of industrial products and of services would have been very restricted. The demand for many industrial products is responsive to reductions in price and to increase in incomes, and process innovations which have reduced labour per unit output by 10 per cent have often been followed by increases in output of more than 10 per cent.

In the production of motor cars, for example, Henry Ford's assembly line greatly reduced the labour required to produce each car, but the reduction in price brought such an increase in demand for cars, that employment in the motor car industry increased. When after the second world war the Japanese car makers made further process innovations in the production of cars which were both capital-saving and labour-saving, there was a further increase in the demand for cars and the labour to produce them. However, in recent years further reductions in labour per unit output by 10 per cent have not been followed by increases in the demand for cars by 10 per cent, and technical change has displaced labour from the production of motor cars.

When cars were first introduced, prices were high, performance poor, and the demand was small. Progressive reductions in price relative to incomes, and improvements in reliability, then led to a rapid growth in the market for cars. During this phase the employment of labour increased. But as markets gradually saturated the rate of market growth fell off, and percentage reductions in labour per unit output made possible by technical changes, started to exceed percentage increases in output. Such a "life-cycle" in the demand for labour is not restricted to the motor-car industry, and if there had not been a flow of new products, the growth in industrial employment would have been much less.

New products which create new markets, or which induce a larger expansion of particular markets than the older products were capable of doing, extend the demand for labour. A sufficient supply of new products at the right times could therefore offset, or more than offset, the fall in the demand for labour, resulting from labour-saving innovations in agriculture and in industrial products which had passed through the rapid-growth phase in their life-cycles. Put in that way, the future of employment in industry depends on the balance between process and product innovations.

There are times when product innovations, and process innovations during the rapid-growth phase of products introduced earlier, increase the demand for labour more than process innovations when mature industries reduce their demand for labour. Such was the position in the 1950s and 1960s. But there is no mechanism in the market-system to ensure that the labour-creating and labour-displacing effects of technical change are always kept in balance. Currently we are suffering from the effects on employment of a fall in product innovations relative to labour-saving process innovations. This has happened periodically in industrial countries when imbalances in the innovation process caused technological unemployment. In the past such imbalances have not lasted much more than ten years, and there is a considerable debate at the moment on whether there will soon be a revival of labour-creating innovations.

Satiety

Before considering this issue there are two other matters to be considered. The first is the reduction in hours of work. The second is the increase in the proportion of labour employed and the signs of a fall in the proportion employed in industry in the most advanced industrial countries.

The hours of work per week and weeks of work per year have come down in the industrialized countries, and the years spent in the labour force have also come down as the average ages of entry to the labour market have risen, and the average ages of retirement fallen. Weekly hours for male workers have fallen by 30 per cent in the last hundred years, and hours of work through the whole working life by almost 50 per cent. For women the reduction in "life hours" has been less because their years in the labour force have risen with the increased employment of married women.

This reduction in hours is due to the decisions of workers to take part of the increase of productivity in the form of shorter hours, and to the effects of higher real incomes on family and government expenditure on education and pension schemes. There has been a trend reduction of 30 per cent in hours of work per year for each 10 per cent increase in output per worker. The decisions to work shorter hours have the effect of keeping incomes and production below the levels that the new technologies could achieve.

In an essay "On the Economic Possibilities for our Grandchildren", J.M. Keynes discussed the implications of what he described as a growing gap between our capacity to produce more goods and our desire to consume more goods. He discussed the implications of the inherited work ethic which, as mentioned earlier, the Rev. Roger Clarke discussed 50 years later, but Keynes doubted whether the problem would become serious before the year 2030 when, "to keep the old Adam at bay" we would share what work there would still be needed as widely as possible and work three hours a day. If increases in productivity and incomes were raised again to the levels of the 1950s, we could reach that Keynesian state by 2030, but at current rates of increase in productivity and income it will take much longer.

The reduction of hours with increases in productivity is not a smooth process, and when the actual reduction is less than the reduction to be expected from increases in productivity there will be a tendency for unemployment to rise. But that does not explain any part of current unemployment. Recent reductions in hours have certainly kept pace with the reductions to be expected from increases in labour productivity at rates of trade-off between more leisure and more income that operated in the last thirty years. There have been many proposals to increase employment by reducing hours, but further reductions in hours would only add to employment if hourly rates of pay did not increase more than current increases in product per hour. Significant reductions in hours to increase employment would therefore entail reductions in take-home pay.

Services

Employment in the services includes education, libraries, the health services, central and local government, banks, insurance companies and retail and wholesale distribution. Since 1870 such employment has risen from 25 per cent to 66 per cent of the labour force in the USA, from 35 to

60 per cent in Britain, from 20 per cent to 50 per cent in Germany, and from 12–15 per cent to 55 per cent in Japan. That increase reflects the change in patterns of expenditure with increases in wealth, and the growth in education, research and advisory services required to sustain economic growth.

However this great growth of employment in the services is a major factor in current fears for the future of employment. For, it is often asserted, recent developments in microprocessors and telecommunications have made possible major labour-saving activities in the services sector—in banks, insurance companies, shops, warehouses, central and local government offices, and even in education. This fear for the future is reflected in the dotted lines in the diagram.

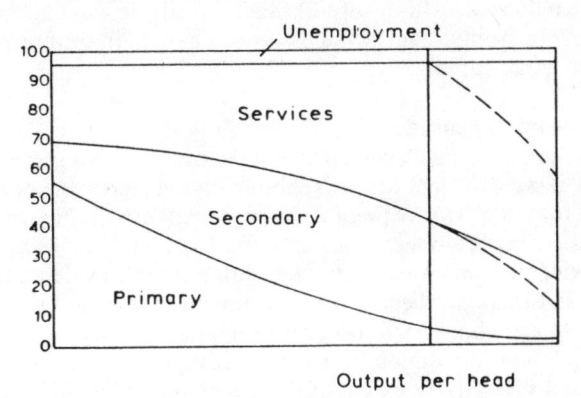

Percentage employment of the labour force

The solid lines give a rough indication of past changes in the distribution of labour between sectors as levels of output per worker increase, and of what the distribution will be if past trends are sustained. Unemployment in the solid line is drawn at a constant 4 per cent, which is the long-term average although there have been substantial annual fluctuations. The broken lines reflect fears for the future of employment relative to the current hours of work.

If, for a correspondingly small increase in output per capita, unemployment did rise to 40 per cent, as at the extreme right in the diagram, it would imply a marked fall in labour-extending relative to labour-saving innovations, and a failure to adjust hours of work. Suppose that while unemployment rose from the 4 to 40 per cent pictured in the graph, output per head would rise by 20 per cent. That would imply almost a doubling in output per worker employed. For in the first situation 96 per cent of the labour force produced x, and in the second situation 60 per cent of the labour force would produce $1.2x$. But such a sustained level of unemployment would be inconsistent with the past responses of workers to increases in productivity. Even at the average post-war rate of trade-off between additional income and additional leisure, there would be a reduction in hours—and so a reduction in unemployment of below 40 per cent. A major reduction in labour-extending product innovations relative to labour-saving process innovations would probably change the trade-off between additional income and additional leisure and increase the proportion of productivity increase taken in the form of leisure. The decline in hours required to reduce unemployment from the notional 40 per cent to 4 per cent would be almost 50 per cent. If hours at the beginning were 38, such a reduction to about 20 would take us near to the 15 hours of work in 2030 predicted by Keynes in his essay of 1930. Yet such a reduction in hours of sharing the available work evenly would not be easy to bring about if the assumed changes in output per man-hour took place rapidly.

A tilt to technical change?

There is certainly a widespread fear at the moment that there has been a tilt in technical change towards labour-saving technologies and that chips and robots will make possible large increases in output per person-hour in the next few years, thus creating high levels of technological unemployment. I am far from convinced that there is evidence to justify the view that there has been a tilt to technical change and that labour-saving technical change will become dominant.

A fall in labour-creating product innovativeness is a standard feature of depressions. Given the extent of R&D activities, I would be surprised if there were not a recovery in product innovation relative to process innovation, with an increase in both. Furthermore, if the acceleration of labour-saving technical change had been an important factor in the present recession, there would have been a rise in annual productivity increases per employed worker. In fact, there was a decline in annual productivity increases which set in before the marked increases in unemployment in the seventies.

It is easy to give excessive emphasis to the role of technical change in the current depression. Other factors of importance were the collapse of the Bretton Woods system of orderly changes in exchange rates, the sharp increase in the prices of grain and oil in the early seventies, the end of the money illusion as a damping factor in wage and salary bargaining and price decisions, and the shift in the objectives of fiscal and monetary policies as a consequence of the acceleration of inflation in the second half of the seventies.

In August 1971, the US government suspended the convertability of the dollar with gold. This followed the fall in the US gold reserves and the unwillingness of the countries with large surpluses, notably the

Federal Republic of Germany and Japan, to make appropriate revaluations of their currencies. The US dollar was formally devalued in December 1971. There was an attempt at that time to restore the Bretton Woods system of stable exchange rates, but the further devaluation of the dollar in 1973 and the floating of the Swiss Franc, the Yen, the Deutschmark and the Lira signalled the collapse of that system.

In 1972, following new political initiatives for cooperation, the US made large sales of grain to Russia at a time when reserves of grain had fallen to low levels. The price of grain, which in the US had been kept stable for many years, rose from $2 a bushel to $3.80 in 1973 and to $4.90 in 1974. The price of oil had not been kept stable. Between 1950 and 1973 the price had risen by 90 per cent (40 per cent relative to gold). And then in 1974 OPEC trebled the price of crude oil and created a substantial balance of payments problem. But that did not end the OPEC contribution to the recession—prices were forced up again in 1979 and 1980 until the price was about twice that of 1978.

Increases in the price of food, oil and gold created strong inflationary expectations. The long period of high growth rates created expectations of annual increases in living standards which had become excessive for the growth rates in output per worker of the sixties and still more excessive for the lower growth rates of the seventies. But inflationary expectations added to the extent of wage and salary claims and gave a further impetus to inflation. In Britain consumer prices doubled in the 20 years after 1950, but more than doubled in the five years after 1974.

In response to the acceleration of inflation and to the balance of payment problems created by the marked increases in oil prices, most governments modified their fiscal and monetary policies. To prevent in the first instance further increases in the rate of inflation, and then to reduce the rate of inflation, governments decided not to increase money supplies sufficiently to accommodate the prevailing rates of increase in costs (including salaries and wages). This change in policy led to an initial increase in unemployment, although in countries such as Britain—unlike Japan and later the US—unions, professional associations, and businesses did not adjust wage, salary and price policies to the new fiscal and monetary policies, with the growing unemployment.

During times of severe unemployment there are always proposals to reduce the supply of labour. The supply of labour could be reduced by raising the average age of entry to the labour market, reducing the average age of retirement, persuading married women that their place is in the home, and reducing hours of labour.

Reductions in the hours of labour in recent years have at least kept pace with the trend in reduction expected from the relation between reductions in hours of work and reductions in labour per unit output. Further reductions would only increase employment if they were in the nature of short-time working; and so far only the Swiss trade unions have accepted that work-sharing involves income-sharing.

During the 1930s there were many fields of public and semi-public employment closed to married women. However, due to the increase in the employment of married women during the second world war, subsequently proposals to revive the policies of the thirties have not been taken seriously.

The average age of retirement has fallen in recent years—particularly in the last ten years, which suggests that some of this reduction is a consequence of the depression. Measures to make significant reductions in the age at which workers qualify for full pensions are very expensive, and they do not make much sense at a time when public expenditure is already distended by the rise in payments to the unemployed.

In contrast, increases in the average age of entry to the labour market *do* make sense if they are engaged in education which encourages young people to acquire manual and mental skills and attitudes of mind which add to their productive capacities. The general educational qualifications of the British work force are substantially less than the work forces in Germany, the USA and Japan. Britain's use of information technology and bio-technology to increase growth and competitiveness in internal trade is impeded by shortages of applied scientists, bio- and electronics engineers, technicians and programmers.

Recovery also depends on the creation of a situation where the fiscal and monetary authorities are not forced to choose between reasonable stability of prices and encouragements to growth through Keynesian demand management policies. Even under present conditions wage and salary costs per unit output are rising faster than in most countries which compete with us in international trade, and this impedes recovery. Despite the experience of the 1970s, and the 1980s so far, there is still a widespread belief among members of trade unions that "labour's share" in the national product can be increased through collective bargaining. But for more than short periods, labour's share can only be so increased if the collective bargain includes measures to increase the output/capital ratio, i.e to increase production relative to capital employed.

There were great expectations during the 1950s and 1960s that the increase in government expenditure on higher education in the sciences and technologies, and the increase in government and business expenditure on research and development, would engineer such a large flow of opportunities for innovation that the rate of technical change and innovation would become both greater and more stable than in the past. Rates of innovation did rise in the fifties and sixties but were not sustained at that high level.

The OECD report, *Technical Change and Economic Policy* (1980), contains a proposal for a change in the way governments attempt to promote a stable flow of new technologies. The proposal is that governments give less emphasis to promoting particular new technologies such as Concordes, and more to supporting strategic research and exploratory development work on enabling technologies. The Alvey programme on innovation technology, organized by the Alvey Directorate in the UK Department of Trade and Industry, is one example of such government activity. Such activity could extend technology options, the range of which may be restricted by the dominance of large firms in industrial R&D, and reduce the time lags and risks involved in the introduction of new technologies. The extensions of technology options, and the reductions of the risks always involved in expenditure on the design and development of new technologies, could be particularly valuable in assisting new and small firms.

It is not possible here to develop further comments on this policy. My main conclusions are that current levels of unemployment cannot be explained simply as a consequence of technical change, and that, although there have been mistakes in demand management policies made by governments acting alone and collectively, in such bodies as the International Monetary Fund, it is not possible to ensure continued high levels of employment through even ideal demand management policies. If we are to ensure continued high levels of employment we need to learn how to get a more even flow of innovations, how to reduce periodic imbalances between labour-creating and labour-displacing innovations, and how to contain or prevent cost-push inflationary pressures (which add to problems of income distribution and encourage imports at the expense of exports—without the need to resort to restrictive monetary and fiscal policies.

The Future of the Mixed Economy

DAVID SIMPSON

The classical tradition in the treatment of economic growth contains such distinguished names as Adam Smith, Karl Marx, Allyn Young and Joseph Schumpeter.[1] Unlike its neo-classical counterpart—the theory of steady state growth—the range of variables in the classical theory is broad enough to encompass the diverse topics proposed, and its methods—those of political economy—are sufficiently flexible to handle the major issues which arise. The point of departure in this paper is the most recent exponent of that tradition, Schumpeter, and it will be necessary to begin with a brief summary of his contribution to our understanding of how a modern advanced economy works. This is followed by an account of Schumpeter's predictions of how such an economy could be expected to develop, in particular the trends which he anticipated in attitudes, institutions and forms of organization. The next section of the paper suggests reasons why the post-war trends in the advanced economy, correctly foreseen by Schumpeter, may now be slowing down or coming to a halt. The changes may even amount to a reversal. There is first a political reason—a desire to preserve the present degree of individual choice, secondly, an economic reason: the unwinding of the present level of the division of labour, and thirdly a technical reason: the nature and rate of progress in technology. Finally, the paper concludes with some reflections on the nature of present tendencies in economic institutions and attitudes and how they may be related to the question of human betterment.

Schumpeter's analysis of economic progress

Schumpeter is perhaps best known for his early work, *The Theory of Economic Development*, published in 1912. However it is on his later work, notably *Capitalism, Socialism and Democracy* (first published in 1942) that I wish to dwell. Here, he expressly approves the correctness of the Marxist vision that capitalism will eventually be replaced by socialism. Schumpeter followed Marx in believing that this change would be brought about by factors endogenous to the capitalist system itself, although he advanced very different reasons from Marx for the disappearance of capitalism. In his view there would be a steady and gradual decomposition: a "quenching of capitalist attitudes and institutions". This idea has echoes of Marx's view that capitalism carries within itself the seeds of its own destruction, but whereas in Marx's case destruction comes about in an abrupt and violent collision between the material and political forces, in Schumpeter's view destruction is slow and moves through intangibles. The transition is painless and indeed the date of transition may not be clearly marked.[2] In both cases, however, capitalism is destroyed by its own success.

The biggest single factor in the decline of capitalism is the decline in the motivation of the entrepreneur. The modern corporation, itself a product of the capitalist process, "socializes the bourgeois mind". The modern corporation executive acquires something of the psychology of the salaried employee working in a bureaucratic organization. The increasing size of firms knocks out the notion of property or of freedom of contract: the figure of the proprietor, and with it the specifically proprietary interest, vanishes from the picture. The labour contract is impersonal, stereotyped and bureaucratic. "The capitalist process takes the life out of the idea of property." In Schumpeter's view, this means that the political structure of society is profoundly changed by the elimination of a host of small and medium-sized firms.

In the last year of his life, 1949, Schumpeter looked at developments in the economies of the United Kingdom[3] and the United States[4] and perceived the continuation of the tendencies which he had identified in 1942. Indeed, he went so far as to predict the trend of events in the following decades.

He foresaw that what he called "social democracy" (or the mixed economy, as we should now call it, or again, "operating the capitalist engine in the labour interest") could only be a transient phase in the economic organization of an advanced society since it lacked the discipline of the forces prevailing in the traditional market economy or the sanctions of a Soviet-type planned economy. Activities which no longer have an economically useful function are automatically eliminated by competition in the market economy. In the command economy, when recognized, they are eliminated by decree. But in a mixed economy, it is frequently possible for those who have a vested interest in uneconomic activities to use the political process to protect and thus to perpetuate such activities.

For its long-term survival, the mixed economy would therefore have to rely on individual self-denial. But to an extent not envisaged even by Schumpeter, in the modern consumer society of the advanced countries of the world (the OECD countries), self-indulgence has taken the place of self-discipline and self-denial. Agents would have to act in the interests of the economy as a whole, rather than in their own material interest. It should be emphasized that this is not just a question of the consumption of private goods. There is an equally insistent demand for the collective provision of goods such as medical care and defence services, as well as the whole range of social security benefits, as indicated by the continuing budget problems of the advanced countries. Consequently, it appears unlikely that the mixed economy could survive for long as a viable form of economic organization. Faced with an increasing proportion of uneconomic activities, the political pressures for change would become irresistible.

Thus Schumpeter anticipated that there would be a gradual drift—a deterioration in his opinion—of the market economy towards a planned economy. There would be no sharp upheaval, no discontinuity of events in practice, but for the analytically minded observer he suggested that the watershed in this transition from capitalism to socialism would be marked by what he called "the socialization of the labour market", which we would today call the establishment and acceptance of a permanent statutory incomes policy.

Since the second world war, there have been significant developments in the organization of the economies of the advanced countries, common to all of them. Apart from the historically high rate of growth in output, there has been an increasing concentration in the size of distribution of firms, notably in the manufacturing industries, the growth of corporate forms of organization at the expense of the family firm, nationalization of many sectors of the economy, great expansion of state provision of medicine, education and social services, various experiments in the introduction of incomes policy, and in general a greater degree of intervention and regulation by governments in the market economy than ever before.

While Schumpeter seems correctly to have anticipated the trends in the advanced countries in the thirty years following his death, when we look today at the situation through his analysis it seems as if these trends are in the process of being arrested. Schumpeter himself would not have been surprised. He was at pains to emphasize that he was making no dogmatic predictions concerning the long-run and that any tendency could be halted or even reversed at any time. In this respect, Schumpeter's view of historical evolution is similar to that of his fellow Austrians, and quite distinct from Marxist determinism.

There are three major reasons why it seems that the post-war drift towards a planned economy in the advanced countries may have been stopped. First of all, the citizens of the advanced countries (whilst Schumpeter addressed himself solely to the US and the UK, I am generalizing these remarks to the OECD countries as a whole) have had the learning experience of more than thirty years of this drift. While they have welcomed the collective provision of such commodities as medical and defence services and they have pressed for the extension of the range of social security benefits so that few governments of these countries have escaped apparently intractable budget balancing problems, they have also experienced the consequences of certain movements in the direction of a planned economy, viz. the establishment of state monopolies, the growth of the central government bureaucracy and the extension of personal taxation and government controls and regulations relating to their personal economic activity.

In particular, most of the advanced countries have experienced since the war periods of statutory restraint on wages and sometimes other incomes, whether under the name of pay pauses, pay freezes, wage guidelines, or whatever. While all of these attempts have been temporary, they have been generally unpopular.[5] At least in the United Kingdom neither major political party has dared to declare that, if elected, they would adopt such policies. Groups of people, like individuals, do undergo a learning process. Indeed, it may be said that one of the characteristics of the democratic political process is that it is a learning process.

The conclusion that I would draw from the history of the past thirty years in the advanced countries is that the population of these countries has decided that incomes policies are an unacceptable restriction on their individual or collective freedom to bargain in the labour market, and that a truly major economic catastrophe leading to a continuing foreseeable decline in their living standards would be necessary before they would be willing to surrender the degree of freedom which they enjoy at present in the labour market. A similar "learning process" argument applies to their political attitude to state monopolies, the bureaucracy, taxation and controls. While people are eager to have the benefits of the welfare state, they have learned that these services also have costs, and they are politically concerned that these should be minimized.

Unwinding the division of labour

Since before the time of Adam Smith, the progress of the advanced countries has proceeded by means of an ever-increasing degree of specialization or division of labour. Indeed, the whole economic development of both the advanced and the developing countries can be regarded as an unfolding of the degree of the division of labour as traditional activities are broken up into increasingly specialized functions to form new industries. Technical progress is intimately related to this process, since, together with the size of the market, it provides the opportunity for taking the division of labour one step further.[6]

As the division of labour proceeds further, however, its costs increase whilst its benefits become less apparent. In the advanced countries today there is what Galbraith has called a diminishing urgency of wants, brought about by a combination of higher levels of consumption of privately purchased material goods and services together with a high level of collective provision of goods and services including widespread social security benefits. It is easy to see therefore why the utility of further extensions of the division of labour, namely high material output, should become less important.

The costs of increasing the division of labour are several. First there is the familiar problem of alienation. By means of specialization in technical progress a worker is typically denied a creative work-role. This of course can be mitigated by the fact that technical progress has been able to eliminate many dirty, menial, dangerous and physically exhausting tasks, and that the conferment of increased status together with higher real wages may compensate for the loss of self-esteem which the worker might otherwise suffer. Secondly, as the division of labour is extended, there are an increasing number of intermediaries between the primary stage of production and the point of final consumption. Since intermediation invariably involves a human agent, and since the price of labour rises relative to other commodities in the course of economic development, it follows that, for most commodities, the total transactions costs, when summed over each stage of intermediation, become over time an increasing proportion of the total costs of production.

Thirdly, the ever-extending chain of interdependence which arises from specialization in a money economy increases the vulnerability of the whole system to disturbance, since the chain is only as strong as its weakest link. The uncertainty which is enhanced by this circumstance dampens risk-taking and thus investment.

Fourthly, there are the social as well as the economic costs of disturbance induced by a further step in the division of labour: these include the costs of unemployment and retraining as well as job-search.

The diminishing utility and increasing costs of continuing further extensions of the divisions of labour in the advanced countries suggest that the process may be slowing down or even coming to a halt. This is not to say that specialization in a technical sense is diminishing; there are after all many new products and new processes coming into existence, but rather that a smaller and smaller proportion of the total available labour is being supplied to the labour market.[7]

It is not simply a question of increased time being devoted to leisure; it is that an increased amount of labour is being applied outside the market, to creative and satisfying forms of work inside or outside the home, including voluntary work and public interest activities, as well as do-it-yourself recreational work, and hobbies.

The shrinking of the market economy and the development of the home economy have a number of important implications. One is that it becomes possible for the individual to opt out of much organized economic activity. This will make less likely the realization of the classical forms of socialism for two reasons. First, attitudes are likely to change towards more self-sufficiency of the family or household group if not the individual (a reversion to peasant-like attitudes). Secondly, a planned economy assumes a high degree of the division of labour within society. Without such an extensive division of labour, planning must be less than comprehensive and control less complete.

Another implication is greater stability for the household or family unit. The "home economy" may involve several members of the household in cooperative activity which is productive, but not necessarily all of which is destined for the market. This may not only have a favourable effect on youth unemployment but equally importantly restores the unity of labour, of which the division of labour is so destructive, together with the psychological benefits which go with it.[8]

The effect of new technologies

As indicated above, the tendency of the market economy to shrink at the expense of the home economy is being reinforced by new developments in the fields of technology, particularly in the field of communications, but also to a lesser extent in the field of energy. These developments are making possible the territorial decentralization of production, so that work for the market may increasingly be performed in the individual household or in small family firms rather than within such agglomerations as factories and cities. This again makes a movement towards socialism less likely. It is after all a highly centralized form of economic organization, and it may not be accidental that planned economies have had the greatest difficulty in coping with such highly decentralized industries as peasant agriculture, where the household is the decision-unit.

We noted above Schumpeter's prediction that the increasing concentration of the size of the firm would shift the political balance of society in the direction of socialist attitudes and towards a planned economy. But if, in fact, this process of the elimination of small firms is now being reversed,[9] then one should expect to find, following his view, that the political balance would move away from socialist attitudes and towards a greater reluctance to accept the central planning of economic activity.

The decline in the relative importance of large scale factory production could also account for a major shift in attitudes. Many economic historians believe that a major element creating feelings of social class hostility was the way in which workers were concentrated in factories and were housed in associated blocks of dwellings whether privately, or later, publicly-owned. If these processes are now being reversed, then one should expect, likewise, the abatement of such feelings.

Other developments in communications technology point in a similar direction. They convey the possibility of the individual shopping, carrying out financial transactions, and even working from home.

As well as the decentralization of production from larger to smaller units of production (in the extreme case, the household), there is also the possibility of territorial decentralization of production, a process for which there is already much evidence. There is the continuing drift of population from the cities to the country. Much attention has been paid to the ensuing problems of the declining inner cities, with attendant social problems. However, these influences on attitudes may be overshadowed in their consequences by the broader changes in political attitudes throughout society.

These tendencies we have just identified are the consequences of the specific form or nature of contemporary technical change. There are also some consequences of the speed of contemporary technical change, which in some industries at least is apparently accelerating. In the great debate[10] in the 1930s about the feasibility of establishing a planned economy, the telling point was made by Hayek that it would be technically impossible for a central planning authority to acquire all the information necessary to carry out correct economic decisions as to the quantity and price of each commodity to be produced. This debate was carried out within the theoretical framework, common to both sides, of a static general equilibrium model, i.e. the basic parameters of information concerning wants, resources and technology pertaining to or available to every household and firm in a hypothetical economy were assumed to be unchanging. Recent developments in communications technology might make it possible to overcome Hayek's objection, at any rate for not too large an economy and for unchanging information. But while the technical problems of data transmission and analysis may be said to have been solved, the problem of the collection of fragmentary and uncertain information, whose dimensions are themselves changing, remains.

The response of institutions to changes in technology

The response of all institutions to the effects of change is to resist it. The classical argument in favour of the market economy as a form of organization is not that it realizes or approximates static allocative efficiency (the neo-classical argument), but that it makes such resistance on the part of institutions unavailing. This was Adam Smith's recipe for economic growth. It may be said that the success of the advanced countries in their economic development since the eighteenth century has been due to the flexibility of firms in response to the pressures of change. Whereas in earlier times pressures upon firms for change largely came from the opening of new territories and the development of consumer demand, it now comes primarily from technical progress. The role of institutions in the process of economic growth is just the same in the developing countries and in the planned economies as it is in the advanced countries. In his authoritative quantitative analysis of the barriers to economic growth in the developing countries, Leontief concluded that the effective constraints were not physical ones, such as a scarcity of resources, but institutional ones.[11] Again, it is worth noting that the principal obstacles to the growth of the contemporary Soviet economy appear to be institutional ones.

Menger identified two kinds of institutional change: there were those which were the result of human action but not human design, to which he gave the word organic. Pragmatic institutions, on the other hand, were those which were generated as the result of legislation or other purposeful collective agreement. As an example of organic processes of institutional change brought about by changes in technology we have already noticed the decentralizing effects of changes in communications and energy technology. This will affect such institutions as, for example, the family and the town. But new technology is having its effect not only on communications between production units but within them as well. The increasing automation of the control and organization of the whole manufacturing process, as well as of individual tasks within it, is bringing about not simply a reduction in the direct labour force, but the enhancement of the advantages of mass production of a variety of products at the expense of small-scale economies, the redundancy of traditional craft apprenticeships. These changes can be expected to have far-reaching effects on the attitudes and organization of the work-force and upon the optimal size and organization of firms.

So far as pragmatic changes are concerned, the development of new communications technology (such as satellites, cables and cassettes) has broken the natural monopoly[12] which the pre-existing state of the art had conferred on the communications industry in the advanced countries. These recent changes have caused the US government to legislate for the break-up of the hitherto publicly-regulated but privately-owned monopoly American Telephone & Telegraph (AT&T). The response of the British government has been rather different. It has now passed legislation transforming the British communications industry from a publicly-owned to a privately-owned monopoly. It is not effectively ending the monopoly as such. Whatever may be said in favour of the particular arrangements in the United States nothing at all can be said in favour of the British legislation, since it is based on an apparent failure to distinguish between the form of organization of an industry (i.e. a monopoly or competitive supply) on the one hand, and the form of ownership on the other (i.e. private or public). It may not be too fanciful to attribute this misunderstanding to the absence of a generally accepted contemporary theory of growth for an advanced economy.[13]

Progress in information technology, together with human preferences for greater independence, points to some characteristics, which we have just outlined, of the successor state to the mixed economy. However, these and other developments in technology are also likely to increase the role of government as the provider of security. At the same time, large corporations (whether publicly—or privately-owned) will continue to exist in many sectors of productive activity, where economies of scale and agglomeration justify them. The economic institutions of the successor state are therefore likely to be pluralistic, with strong political rivalry between the bureaucracy of government and of the large corporations on the one hand, and small to medium-sized firms, the home economy, and perhaps the black economy, on the other. The bureaucracy and the corporate sector will represent pressures for security and order and resistance to change, while the other sectors of society will represent pressures for freedom and flexibility in the widest senses of those words.

Conclusions

What does all this mean in terms of social change? In the nineteenth and early twentieth centuries the prevailing form of economic organization—the market economy—permitted the realization of the potential for technical progress, with resulting benefits of higher living standards in the advanced countries. This material progress was not achieved without considerable costs, which flowed directly from the form of organization itself. Now, however, it is possible, following the transitional state of the mixed economy, to envisage a successor state in which the population of the advanced countries will not only have been freed from material poverty, but will also have been freed from the organizational constraints which were necessary to overcome that poverty. While the successor state may be centralized as to its security aspects, in the field of production and consumption (i.e. economic activity) it will be highly decentralized, with consequent benefits for the family and community life.

The notion of economic transition as a turnpike was introduced to us by Dorfman, Samuelson and Solow. Their analysis was confined to strictly quantifiable data concerning capital stock and the composition of output in a growing economy. We can employ a similar metaphor more loosely to describe the progress of human society from the pre-industrial to the post-industrial period. In order to achieve rapid economic growth in the industrial era it was necessary for household independence to be sacrificed so that the advantages of higher productivity obtainable through the extension of the division of labour could be achieved. At the end of the turnpike, once the material benefits of higher productivity have been achieved, households (labour supply units) may be able to revert to the degree of independence which they formerly possessed.

In principle, therefore, we should expect to find that institutional forms could evolve in the successor state to the mixed economy which will make possible the realization of the traditional aspirations of western civilization for the entire population of the advanced countries.

Whether this dramatic potential will be realized is, of course, another question. It is a question which it might be wiser to leave unanswered, were it not for the fact that social change is a central theme of this volume. I therefore feel obliged to make a few remarks on this question by way of conclusion.

Those who have thought and written about the human condition can fairly easily be divided into one or the other of two classes. There are those who believe that human misery is the product of circumstance external to the individual human being, and that therefore, given some appropriate form of economic and social organization, the kingdom of heaven can be built upon earth. In the simplest form of this view, material poverty is by far the greatest, if not the only burden on humanity; it follows that the lifting of this burden will usher in an age of universal happiness. Into this class fall Marx and Rousseau.

Into the second class fall all those who believe that the removal of the burden of poverty will merely make way for other human problems to come to the fore. It is a view expressed by such writers as Forster, Orwell and Huxley. All of these writers foresee that the developments in technology which make possible the abolition of material poverty in human societies will eventually destroy "every vestige of humanity" (in Gerver's words[14]) in the citizens of these societies.

Although few who have experienced them would claim that the availability of eighty television channels represents any contribution to human betterment (rather the reverse, it seems), it is possible to err too much on the side of pessimism. In Pakistan, for example, it is reported that those citizens with TV sets ignore the government-inspired propaganda which dominates all the broadcast channels, and use the sets simply to play their video cassettes, which are freely available. My own view is that the net effect of new developments in technology within our changing political and economic system will be a liberating one, which will alleviate the lot of most people. At the very least, it means that people can be miserable in comfort.

NOTES

1. I am grateful to Robert Crawford and James Walker for their comments on an earlier draft of this paper. It appeared orginally as a Fraser of Allander Institute Discussion Paper No. 32.
2. See page 30.
3. See the preface to the third English edition of *Capitalism, Socialism and Democracy*, London, 1949.
4. See "The March into Socialism", *American Economic Review*, May 1950.
5. Ironically, the trade unions have been the strongest source of opposition to incomes policies in the United Kingdom. In this respect, they are blocking the road to socialism.
6. All this was the subject of the presidential address to Section F of the 1928 meeting of the British Association in Glasgow. A. Young, "Increasing Returns and Economic Progress", *Economic Journal*, December 1928.
7. When the supply of labour is measured by hours offered through a working life, the reduction in the supply in the UK between 1870 and 1980 is almost 50 per cent. See Bruce Williams, "Technology Policy and Employment", discussion paper, the Technical Change Centre, London, 1983.
8. Ref. Simone Weil, *The Need for Roots*.
9. It may be asked: what is the empirical evidence for the assertion that a process of deconcentration is under way? The evidence is necessarily fragmentary. I would concede that many of the older manufacturing industries may be becoming more concentrated, but this process must surely be outweighed by the growth of the services sector. Despite the recession and the uncertain investment outlook, the formation of new companies in Scotland (which are virtually entirely small companies) is at an all time high.
10. O. Lange and F.M. Taylor, *On the Economics of Socialism,* Chicago, 1938. F.A. Hayek ed., *Collectivist Economic Planning,* London, 1935.
11. W.Leontief ed., *The Future of the World Economy,* Oxford, 1975.
12. Rothbard and others believe that the only true monopoly is one which is protected by state legislation, since all unprotected "natural" monopolies will, in time, be eliminated by the competition of alternative modes or technologies. The critical question is: how long will this time period be?
13. See D. Simpson, *The Political Economy of Growth,* Oxford, 1983, Chap. 3.
14. I am grateful to Elizabeth Gerver for drawing to my attention E. M. Forster's short story *The Machine Stops*, from which a quotation appears in her contribution, "The Social Geography of Computers," which appears in the forthcoming book: T.F. Carbery ed., *Essays on the Development of Information Technology in Scotland,* Aberdeen.

PART II

Current Employment Policies and Assumptions

A View from Industry

JOHN DAVIDSON

This is the age of the decline and fall of the mass employment empire. Huge work-forces largely engaged in repetitive, easily acquired skills are rapidly being replaced by equipment that can perform the same tasks more accurately and far more quickly. But if mass employment is not to be replaced by mass unemployment there must be dramatic changes in the way work is organized.

The work pattern of the majority of Scots has evolved from the industrial revolution. The same is true of every industrial country both East and West. And, with varying degrees of success, it has been adopted or adapted by the emerging countries of the third world. It is a pattern that is common to those who work in manufacturing industry, in the service sector, in wholesaling and retailing and in administration. Our work pattern creates an expectation—even a standard—of a life of some 100,000 working hours in an organization framework tailored to provide maximum mutual support and the optimum utilization of buildings and equipment. Large work-forces often numbered in tens of thousands at a single location could only function effectively if individuals worked closely with each other with a degree of interdependence. This imposed constraints of working time and of social attitudes which may rapidly become obsolete.

There is nothing new in advanced technology and in the changes it imposes on economics and societies. The late 1700s and early 1800s experienced an extremely dramatic explosion in the way in which economic life was organized. The social earthquake associated with it affected every element in society—not least the religious. More recently the last hundred years have seen the virtual disappearance of agriculture as a significant employer of labour in Britain. In the late nineteenth century it employed one-quarter of the work-force. It now employs under 3 per cent yet the production of the industry has greatly increased—and that agricultural work-force has moved elsewhere.

The difference between those earlier cycles of change and the one we are now facing is the rate at which it is happening. Previously the change, while rapid, could be absorbed at a national level over a generation or so. Any cycle longer than a generation allows new skills to be acquired by the younger entrants to the labour market, it provides for sufficient employment in declining industries to give work for those closer to retirement, it enables housing and other social infrastructure to keep pace with the new needs. In the past it even enabled our education system to catch up. It was not easy but changes in other spheres could keep broadly in step with technology. That is no longer the case. Technology is moving so rapidly that it is hard for those involved to keep in touch with what is happening, let alone provide time for the multiple adjustments necessary for everyone else to keep in step.

So the shock waves of change wash across the economy and through society far faster and much more frequently than in the past. No thoughts of how to cope with the unemployment implications will be in any way relevant to the problem without fully grasping the changing nature of change.

A further element affecting employment in Europe is the growing tendency for traditional markets to manufacture themselves more and more of the products that they were accustomed to provide.

Britain exports a higher production of its gross domestic products than any other manufacturing nation. So we are especially vulnerable to nationalistic trading policies adopted by our traditional markets. And we are also more at risk by failures to compete effectively at an international level.

The 1973 and particularly the 1979 oil crises seriously disrupted world trading patterns and employment suffered accordingly.

In the UK the pressure was compounded by a distorted valuation of sterling based on the assessment placed on North Sea oil during a period of world oil instability. Further damage was done by a consistently poor competitive performance by the manufacturing sector over an extended period.

So while technological change is a prime factor behind rising unemployment, it is not the only one. Market-related issues are equally important and part of the solution will lie in economic action.

The great temptation is to suggest simplistic remedies in the face of the worst unemployment since the war. Rather, there are a number of trends that might be encouraged which together would reflect the changing context and perhaps reduce the worst social consequences of unemployment.

For most people employment is a means to an end. Wages paid in return form the principle source of income of families of working age. But employment structures have increasingly been seen to be too rigid to meet the changing market and technological context.

Hence work and income ought to be policy objectives rather than employment levels alone. That implies significant increases in the number of self-employed, a more effective tax and social security system and recognition of voluntary effort. And with this should go an awareness that we have one of the highest activity rates (the proportion of those seeking work in each age band) in the world—a significant statistical factor in the unemployment totals.

The Confederation of British Industry has strongly and consistently urged a programme of public sector capital expenditure on roads, water supplies, sewerage systems, railways and other essential services. Not only would it provide more jobs but it would cut the costs faced by industry and commerce and thereby indirectly promote employment.

But those are essentially short-term measures.

It is often argued that a shorter working life would spread wider a given national total of work. But there is a presumption that people will individually accept the lower remuneration either on a lifetime or on a weekly basis that must accompany such a policy.

And much of the evidence available suggests that neither a shorter working week nor early retirement necessarily leads to surplus work going to those unemployed. Frequently it is those already in work who see an opportunity to extend their earning capacity by taking a second job or working after their official retirement (especially if it is an enforced early one).

But the principal criticism of shorter working days or years is the assumption both that work will be available and that the given level of work on which the concept is based is immutable. The former belief is complacent and the latter defeatist.

The demand for our labour whether we are in manufacturing, the service industries, the professions or self-employed is not enough to keep us all gainfully employed. Put another way, in a very competitive world we are unable to persuade customers or clients to buy us all. Much of our problem is economic. We charge too much for our time and effort, and our inefficiencies load the cost to the customer. But even more, our difficulty is a marketing one.

Nationally we are not selling the goods or providing the services that customers seek.

But individually the level of training and expertise that collectively creates the product the customer is seeking is below that of the individual in the countries with which we are competing. And that is essentially a matter of training and education. Education improves an individual's adaptability to changing circumstances and enables him to be a beneficiary rather than a victim of technical advance.

There has rightly been much official encouragement for the smaller firm, but individual enterprise in Scotland still has severe hurdles to overcome in coping with personal attitudes. It really should be much more acceptable to be self-employed or to set out alone on building up a business. Individuals would have a job in which they could be very flexible in meeting the demands of the market. And the same advantages would accrue to those employed by small firms able to respond quickly to changing conditions.

In not tolerating the present levels of unemployment I cannot accept that we are bound within some conceptual limit of work available. We will only ensure a job—employed or self-employed—for ourselves and more importantly for our children if we ensure that individually our competence will enable us to sell ourselves.

Otherwise we shall increasingly be forced to carry the burden of other people's unemployment—a load that our children would increasingly have to bear. They will be even less willing than we to accept it.

Labour and New Technology: a New Strategy?

LYNNE AMERY[1]

It requires no violent stretch of the imagination to conceive that in the near future there will be little work other than machine making and machine minding. If the workers could secure a fair share of the advantages of labour-saving machinery its introduction might become an entire blessing. Most, if not all, the evils induced by lack of interest in monotonous employment would quickly disappear.[2]

Technological change is the great alchemist. Where once was the tedium of work and the threat of unemployment, there is now the prospect of enriched employment for the few and the leisured society for the many. Where once was the stagnant economy of strike-ridden manufacturing, the sun is now rising over the team spirit of Silicon Glen and the service sector. The disabled and the elderly are promised technological aids to alleviate their problems. It's not all space invaders and digital watches. The age of the microchip is hailed as the age of liberation.

Such was the prevalent view also in the 1890s when the words above were written. Mechanization in the engineering trades held similar promises for trade unionists. It is unfortunate that the lessons of history are quickly forgotten. The 1890s witnessed rising unemployment, disunity between engineering workers, and defeat for the unions following the 1897-8 lockout. This was the outcome of a union campaign for the 8-hour day and an agreement on demarcation to limit the introduction of unskilled workers.

Clearly it would be folly to suggest an "iron law of history" by which technological change is forever a Battle of Wounded Knee with the unions standing in for Custer. But it must be acknowledged that there is nothing inherently liberatory about technology. In this paper we argue that technological change must be considered in its political context. This takes full account of the forces which determine the direction of change. It demands a strategy which transcends the sectional concerns of trade unionists in negotiating new technology in the work-place. The central argument is that change must not be reacted to; it must not be divorced from the wider process of restructuring. Rather, the initiative must be seized to create an alternative social vision in which the potentials of technology are liberated from purely economic forces.

Forging this alternative requires new political objectives and alliances. The 1890s saw the emergence of the "new unionism" organizing the unskilled, promoting internationalism and building support for a new radical politics. This example must be applied to the 1980s. As we explain, the foundation is there—it's up to us to build on it.

Technology—a question of power

It is often claimed that technology is neutral—its development is powered by the motor of science which drives it along the unalterable path of innovation and discovery. If we ask "why do we have the motor car?" the answer comes back: "Because after the invention of the wheel and the internal combustion engine it was the next logical step of applying the technology." But why do motor cars corrode and wear out after a few years? "Because", the answer comes back, "we've not yet discovered appropriate alloys or methods of construction." Why not? "Because we haven't been asked to."

Car owners the world over would clearly support such a request, but there's one major obstacle standing between the technologists and the needs of the public. It's the people who pay the technologists. We don't have long-life cars because the vehicle manufacturers would sell fewer of them. The technology of transport has thus proceeded in a direction dictated by the needs of manufacturers to sell more vehicles. The needs of the consumer are thus largely ignored, or transformed through the power of advertising.

This example illustrates the problem in seeing technology as "neutral". On the contrary it has the potential to develop in any number of directions. Its eventual path is determined by the problems that it is called on to solve. Those who control its development are those who specify the problems. In an industrial society problems are specified by industry and determined ultimately by market forces. So it is not human need but profit-making need which is the "power behind the button".

There is nothing original in this argument, but it is necessary to restate it before we analyse the role of micro-electronic technology. It is worth noting that the most eloquent exposition of this viewpoint is that of Mike Cooley.[3] There are two implications which follow from the argument. First of all, liberating the potential of technology to meet human need is clearly a political process. Second, this process should not be limited to the control of the institutions of power. Given that technology has been shaped by the needs of an industrial system in which power is centralized in progressively fewer corporations and institutions, the form of technology reinforces such a centralization. It is therefore necessary to redesign technologies as well as the democratic structures which will determine their development in the future.

From this analysis we can consider the new technology of microelectronics. What are the needs of industry which it is answering? In short, it is the fundamental need to restructure and maintain profitability. Periodically industry goes into recession as demand and profits fall. It can only pull itself out by restructuring—getting rid of less profitable sectors, cutting its costs and reorganizing production. In order to restructure new problems are posed, many of which require a technical solution. How can labour input be reduced? Greater automation. How can administration be more efficient? New computer control systems and communications. Economic recovery is generated by new industries providing the technological infrastructure to enable this transformation.

The current phase of restructuring involves a number of inter-related processes. Firstly, production is increasingly internationalized. Firms do this for various reasons including making use of cheap, unorganized labour and creating economies of scale. New technological developments have enabled this to increase in scope and pace. Second, new production processes have fragmented and deskilled large areas of work, while at the same time creating new skills and job enrichment for a narrow stratum of the work-force.

Taken together these developments have led to a "new international division of labour" in some industries, particularly electronics.[4] For example, in Silicon Valley, California, research and development for microprocessors is carried out by well-paid, highly skilled workers. But most of the manufacturing process is undertaken in Southeast Asia by a low-wage, female work-force.

This restructuring depends on the maintenance of such low-wage areas both in the third world and developed countries. It also requires that opposition to the changes by those workers displaced is headed off. Central to the whole process, therefore, are strategies to neutralize trade unionism and increase control of labour. Throughout the world unions have been thrown on to the defensive. In some countries, overt repression has taken place. In others, such as Britain, there has been a pincer movement of legislative control on the one hand and measures to bypass unions on the other. These include the quality circle movement and shifting production to "greenfield" sites where there are few traditions of trade unionism.

There can be little doubt that international restructuring is the greatest challenge yet to face organized labour. It is creating a new technological and economic infrastructure suited purely to the needs of industry in maintaining profitability. If this requires areas of sweated labour, mass unemployment and military repression, then so be it. If it produces a resurgence of nationalism and racism to encourage competition and justify the new global underclass of workers, then that too is necessary. To confront the "inevitability" of these, often disturbing, developments necessitates new approaches and strategies and, most importantly, a new vision of a democratic, humanitarian alternative.

However, the problem for labour is that it is neither structured nor ideologically prepared to meet this challenge: the problem is global, but labour's perspectives are national; solutions need to be assertive, but labour is traditionally reactive; issues are linked, but unions deal with problems in a fragmented way; a vision is needed, but much of labour's ideological baggage is unsuited to such a task, oscillating between pragmatism and a simplistic notion of "class struggle". These problems become clear when labour's responses to the key elements of restructuring are examined. In Britain the major manifestations of the restructuring have been: new technologies in the work-place; new "hi-tech" firms; mass unemployment.

Problems of strategy

The Trades Union Congress report "Employment and Technology" published in 1979 set the framework for union strategies on new technology. The main part of this was technology agreements (TAs) between unions and management to ensure that technological change is a negotiable issue preventing major job losses and other "damaging effects on the work-force". With hundreds of such agreements having been made it is possible to assess their worth in protecting the interests of trade union members. Recent research by the Technology Policy Unit at Aston University examined a hundred TAs.[5] This concluded that most agreements fell far short of protecting jobs, cutting working time or securing regrading, retraining and information. Divisions between unions have been exploited on the employers' side. In the vast majority of cases it has been single-union agreements which have been made, largely with white-collar unions. Perhaps the major problem with the TA strategy is that they only benefit workers in a strong bargaining position. Especially during a recession this imposes a strict limit on the occupational groups and work-places in which they can be introduced.

The information technology industry is hailed as the saviour of the British economy. Despite the highly questionable nature of this assertion it is true that recent years have seen new electronics firms established in Britain. One of the centres for this activity is the so-called "Silicon Glen" in southern Scotland. This has been a focus for investment by multinational companies such as Motorola, IBM, Wang and DEC. A characteristic of these firms has been their non-union policy—only one in three Scottish hi-tech workers is in a union, and some sectors such as semi-conductors are completely non-union.[6] Personnel policies are designed to prevent any basis for collective organization from recruitment, where predominantly young, female workers are taken on through payment, where wages are individualized, to the company's ideology where a team spirit is fostered using techniques such as quality circles.

There has been little concerted effort on the part of unions to confront this problem. On the contrary, disunity has abounded. The electricians' union, the EETPU, has taken the controversial step of trying to negotiate what it describes as "no-strike agreements" with such firms. This has led to a major row between the EETPU and other unions who interpret this as company unionism. This, of course, is denied by the electricians, but it is a denial which is hard to accept after their recent statement about applying to join the Confederation of British Industry. Regardless of the pros and cons of no-strike agreements, the electricians' "go-it-alone" policy has had the effect of undermining unity between unions at the very time that it was most needed.

This fragmentation in the identification of problems and the development of strategy is most acute in terms of the global dimension of restructuring, and highlights the fundamental contradiction within trade unionism. It may be the stuff of stirring songs, of heartfelt resolutions and slogans, but as a guiding principle of action, internationalism has always had a distinctly hollow ring to it. This is especially the case today. Trade union internationalism has for years had to cope with the problems of bureaucracy, political division and intrigue.[7] This has prevented the development of effective responses to multinationals and changes in the international economy. Unions have been preoccupied with national economic concerns. Because of this labour internationalism has merely reflected and reinforced the divisions between competing national economies.[8] This preoccupation with economic concerns, or "economism", has been a barrier to an effective internationalism, without which advances at a national level are limited. Two implications follow. First, there is an urgent need to supplant economic with wider concerns which go further than workplace issues. Second, in order to build support for this, it is necessary to develop discussions at the lowest level of the labour movement.

The challenge of design

It is clearly not the case that there is an ideologically coherent alternative which can instantly replace the present muddled and fragmented responses. But there are emerging initiatives and ideas which can rekindle imagination, thereby providing its basis. These initiatives focus on three main forms of activity: building links between issues and new channels of solidarity; developing workable alternatives in terms of technological and social organization; effecting new forms of communication to stimulate ideas and the exchange of information.

The most significant of these initiatives may be considered here. One more positive response by trade unionists to the loss of jobs was that of the Lucas Aerospace Combine Committee and their alternative corporate plan for socially useful production. This stimulated other initatives by trade unionists elsewhere and the claim of a "new trade unionism in the making".[9] The idea of socially-useful production drew from a long, largely forgotten history in British trade unionism which, for example, had been manifested by workers in the Coventry aircraft industry just after the second world war. Taken up by the peace movement, this has now developed into a wider campaign for the conversion of military to peaceful production. Related to the Lucas initiative has been the resurgence of the cooperative movement since the 1970s.

As well as developing alternative technologies and forms of industrial organization, trade unionists have also begun to evolve new union structures to secure greater solidarity. Again, the idea of shop steward combine committees was given a shot in the arm by Lucas, demonstrating new potentials and applicability. In addition to national combines, the late 1970s also saw a growth in international combines. Over the last few years especially the international activities of rank-and-file unionists have developed from a concern with economic necessity to an interest in the plight of third world workers, from which has arisen concrete acts of internationalism.[10]

An important internationalist innovation has come from the women's movement, the focus of perhaps the most significant ferment of ideas in recent years. Developing new forms of organization among women in the work-place and community took its next logical step with the formation of Women Working Worldwide, a network of women workers and trade unionists concerned to build solidarity between women's struggles in the North and the South.[11] Many of these initiatives mentioned so far have received support from War on Want. This is illustrative of changes which have taken place within the development movement. Most important has been the growing recognition that development in both North and South is linked and that bridges between campaigns must be built.

Many of the examples cited above are concerned mainly with work-related issues. They may be defined in a wider context, but the focus of activity remains the work-place. But movements have arisen in the community which should be considered. Organization amongst tenants has a long history, but given cutbacks in housing programmes and increasing deprivation, their relevance has been sharpened. Campaigns have been launched on housing issues which have had some successes, although clearly much more is to be done. Such organization has also laid the ground for other campaigns, for example to oppose school and hospital closures. Other forms of community action have involved black people, pensioners, and the unemployed. All of these groups over recent years have evolved forms of organization to deal with the problems that they face. This has perhaps gone furthest in black groups. Black people face the problem that many democratic movements, such as unions and political parties, are themselves riddled with racism and thus unable to further the interests of blacks. Their own organizations are not only providing them directly with a "voice", but also act as a campaigning base from which to reform trade unions, etc.

What we have, then, are a variety of responses to the crisis facing people at work and in the community. They reflect the boundless imagination of working people, families and the jobless in looking at problems in a new way and seeing solutions to them. What, perhaps, we are witnessing is the weaving together of a number of diverse threads and the suggestion of a pattern as they intertwine. Certainly it's woolly around the edges, but this reflects flexibility and adaptation. It therefore has the potential to develop a vision of the future based on the re-design of systems—technological, social and economic. Realizing this potential requires coordination in drawing these threads together and providing support of a concrete nature.

Two new forms of organization have arisen to provide this. Local resource centres give such initiatives assistance of a technical nature: undertaking research, helping with publicity and enabling contacts to take place between them. One of the first centres to be established, Coventry Workshop, demonstrates these functions. The Workshop services trade unionists, tenants' associations, women's groups and local campaigns. Tenants' associations have been put in touch with trade unionists in the council's housing department. Trade unionists from different industries formed a network, based at the Workshop, concerned with exchanging information on new technology. Employees in multinationals in Coventry have been put in touch with their counterparts in other countries. Most recently the Workshop provided technical support to the Bitteswell Employment Alliance, a worker cooperative of ex-British Aerospace employees, who are developing socially useful production in the city.

Such resource centres provide local support to campaigns and help in forging links between them. Coventry Workshop itself was instrumental in establishing a further form of organization. Transnationals Information Exchange (TIE) is an international network of resource centres, union groups and researchers. TIE's objective is to stimulate and sustain international responses to the crisis amongst working people, especially concerning multinational companies.

Local resource centres and international networks have responded to the needs of the new initiatives and will continue with their patient work in supporting them. However, perhaps the time has come to embark on a new phase of activity. Over the last few years local authorities have attempted to draw on this experience and energy and have evolved the concept of "Popular Planning". Examples of this are to be found in London, the West Midlands and other metropolitan areas. Important lessons have been learnt, in particular the danger of compromising these initiatives in the interests of political expediency, and the problem of creating an elite group of "popular planners" who supply workers with workers' plans. This has been partly because the threads and experiences have yet to be fully combined in designing new forms of social and technological organization.

What perhaps is needed is an R&D programme to coordinate this design. It would be concerned with developing alternative technologies, new forms of self-managed organizations and, most importantly, training people in the elements of socialized employment and production. Taking the Science Park principle a stage further, what is envisaged is a "People's Park". It is an environment where re-design projects are undertaken to create workable examples of alternative systems. Central to the idea is the open exchange of ideas and approaches and its accessibility. This is important if its educational role is to be realized. Such a centralized resource requires careful planning to ensure that it supplements rather than substitutes local initiative. But it would seem the next logical step in opening up the prospect of real industrial and social democracy.

The new technologies can be liberating, but only if the process of design itself is liberated from narrow criteria. As this paper has attempted to argue, design must encompass all elements of the present industrial system. It must also be a process which draws on people's wider experiences and aspirations. The time has come to create laboratories which can be used to further "Total Design", encouraging diversity and experimentation in every aspect of economic, social and political activity. The 1890s gave us a new political idealism. The task in the 1980s is to recover that idealism in designing a better world.

NOTES

1. The Coventry Workshop was set up in 1975 to carry out research and advisory work within the local trade union, labour and community movement. Lynne Amery attended the Glasgow workshop on behalf of the Coventry Workshop.

2. M. Berg ed., *Technology and Toil*, Humanities Press, 1979, p. 195.
3. *Architect or Bee*, Langley Technical Services.
4. For reasons of brevity any discussions on theoretical interpretations of the new international division of labour have had to be excluded. Those interested should refer to: F. Frobel, J. Heinrichs and O. Kreye, *The New International Division of Labour*, Cambridge, 1980; R. Jenkins, "Divisions Over the International Division of Labour", in *Capital and Class*, Spring 1984; D. Elson and R. Pearson, "Nimble Fingers Make Cheap Workers", *Feminist Review*, No. 7, 1981. See also Stephen Maxwell's contribution to this volume.
5. H. Levie and R. Williams, "User Involvement and Industrial Democracy", 1983, a working paper available from Technology Policy Unit, University of Aston, Birmingham.
6. The policies of electronics manufacturers are reviewed in *Labour Research*, No. 11, Vol. 72, 1983.
7. D. Thomson and R. Larson, "Where Were You, Brother", War on Want, 1978.
8. This argument is extended by W. Olle and W. Schoeller, "World Market Competition", in *Capital and Class*, No. 2, 1977.
9. The Lucas initiative and its implications are discussed in H. Wainwright and D. Elliot, *The Lucas Plan*, Allison and Buzby, 1982.
10. Discussions on this issue are to be found in P. Waterman ed., *For a New Labour Internationalism*, 1984. The journal *International Labour Reports* covers news on such developments.
11. *Women Working Worldwide*, published by War on Want, 1984.

Labour Market Planning: the Role of a State Agency

ROBERT WHYTE

The Manpower Services Commission (MSC) in the UK was set up in 1974 to run the employment and training services previously provided by the Department of Employment. The Commission's main aim has always been to enable the country's manpower resources to be developed fully to promote economic wellbeing and to ensure that each worker has the opportunities and services he or she needs in order to compete satisfactorily in the labour market. I will try to bring together and clarify the main elements of MSC strategies and show how the Commission has responded to recent changes in the levels of activity and structure of the economy.

As the economy has developed over this past decade so also has MSC's response to the emerging problems of unemployment and skill shortages via a range of new programmes and special measures to the extent that MSC's influence on the labour market is now quite significant. More emphasis is being placed on the training role than ever before and within the Employment Service the MSC is becoming particularly sensitive to the needs of special groups, for example the longer-term unemployed and the disabled.

The labour market background

Any manpower strategy, of course, must begin with an appreciation of the labour market. MSC's plans over the last few years have been drawn up against a picture of depressed output and rapidly falling employment. In the most recent period there has been some limited recovery with output and employment beginning again to grow slowly and prospects for the future look brighter than they have done for some time. Nevertheless, there is a strong underlying demographic growth in the population of working age, and this coupled with any encouragement effect arising from higher employment opportunities, will increase labour supply. Unemployment is likely to remain high, therefore, for some time. At present, the broad judgment on which MSC's plans are based is that total unemployment will fall only modestly in Great Britain as a whole over the next five years. Scotland is unlikely to fare any better.

Within the total, two special categories stand out; the young unemployed, and the long-term unemployed. Young people will benefit from any increase in employment opportunities, while in addition there will be some demographic decline over the next few years in numbers of young people in the population of working age. The opposite side of this effect, however, is some worsening of prospects in unemployment in older age groups, as the demographic "bulge" moves on.

In the absence of remedial policies the numbers of long-term unemployed would be likely to go on rising for some time to come. Similarly, within the total there may be worsening durations of unemployment for certain disadvantaged groups.

This sets clearly the tenor of the problem to which MSC's Employment Service will have to address itself.

Nevertheless, although the large-scale fall in demand for labour associated with the recession has tended to dominate labour market analysis and discussion in recent years, there have been at the same time important changes in the economy's requirements for manpower which themselves have required adaptation and innovation in training provision and other labour market services. These have been caused principally by changes in product and process technology, but also by changes in industrial structure in response to changing patterns of domestic and export demand and competition and in response to the growth of the service sectors.

With the prospect of little change in the levels of employment and unemployment in the next few years, the economy is likely to continue to adjust and develop and a number of recent features of labour market change are expected to continue. Of particular importance to Scotland are changes brought about by the rapid growth experienced in new technology-based industries. These changes have taken place in the context of shifts in employment from manufacturing industry to the service sector, and the related longer-term shift from manual to white collar work. A number of recent changes in the structure of the labour market will have particular implications for employment and training services:

(a) First, in terms of the industrial mix of employment, there has been a significant shift in employment from manufacturing and construction industries to service industries. The continuation of this trend will have implications for the scale of training provision by industries in these respective sectors. The MSC for their part, have already given this consideration in their discussions on adult training, while the emphasis of the existing training opportunities programme has, for some time, been moving away from the traditional heavy manufacturing industries.

(b) Second, there has also been a relative shift in the labour force from employment to self-employment. Again, MSC's current provision has considered this development in the labour market and programmes such as the Enterprise Allowance Scheme and the New Enterprise Training Programme have been targeted at potential entrepreneurs.

(c) Third, the proportion of total employment accounted for by part-time jobs is currently at the highest level ever recorded. First indications are that the rise in employment that has now been recorded is entirely due to increasing numbers of part-timers while the number of full-time jobs is still falling. In as much as this might reflect decisions by firms to opt for flexibility in the face of the increasing need for workers it could represent a significant change in the labour market, with implications for the provision of employment and training services.

(d) Fourth, there has been a significant shift in the pattern of skilled employment in recent years. Job gains in the economy have been concentrated in higher level skills, both professional and technical, while job losses have been in unskilled manual jobs and traditional craft skills. Nevertheless, the scale of the loss of unskilled jobs is unlikely to be repeated in the period ahead since this was partly a product of the severity of the recession. Job gains, on the other hand, are likely to continue to be concentrated at the higher skill levels.

More recently, there has been evidence that certain skill shortages have begun to re-emerge despite the continued high levels of unemployment. Most serious are shortages at higher skill levels (technicians and graduates), particularly in electronics and computer innovations and in advanced manufacturing systems. These reflect the strong underlying processes of structural change. This combination of developing shortages and the long time necessary at these levels to train individuals from scratch, seems to emphasize the need to make full use of refresher, upgrading and conversion training, which is of course a central theme in the Commission's proposals for adult training.

The impact of the recession and the need to improve competitiveness have added impetus to the need to reassess training requirements and it is now clearer than ever that an essential contribution to future economic growth will come from a work-force which is well-trained and possesses the requisite skills and expertise. The programmes being introduced by the MSC, principally through the Youth Training Scheme and the Adult Training Strategy, intend to cater for many of the changes and trends that I have just outlined.

Roles and priorities

International evidence confirms only too clearly that in relative terms our labour market performance falls a long way short of what is needed to maintain competitiveness. The aim must be to create and sustain the highly motivated, highly productive, adaptable, and mobile modern work-force which the country needs. This realization is captured comprehensively in the three objectives of the Government's New Training Initiative, which are:

a) First, the modernization of training in occupational skills (including apprenticeships) particularly to replace out-dated age limits and time-serving with training to agreed standards of skill appropriate to the jobs available.
b) Second, better preparation in schools and colleges for working life and better arrangements for the transition from full-time education to work.
c) Third, wider opportunities for adults to acquire and improve their skills.

The Manpower Services Commission's role in this context is twofold. First, it must help people and firms to make the best of present labour market opportunities by the supply of brokerage services and relevant information. It is MSC's intention to make the existing machinery work more smoothly and efficiently and it is in this vein that the Employment Service is currently being reviewed. But, beyond that, there is the realization that, particularly in the training dimension, attitudes must be changed radically to ensure a more positive approach, by both industry and the labour force, towards training and retraining. The Commission must act as a catalyst for change by encouraging and enabling individuals and firms to commit themselves to the necessary investment in new and higher level skills. This can be done, for example, by supplying information, moving obstacles, widening access, demonstrating innovations, and ensuring that training providers supply an efficient and flexible product. In doing all this the Commission has, to some extent, taken upon itself the role of a national training authority.

The Commission has also always had a duty to help individuals who are at a disadvantage in the labour market, and given the apparent prospects for the labour market in the forthcoming period it will be necessary for the Commission to pursue social as well as wider economic objectives.

Policy development priorities

I have not attempted to describe or list the entire gamut of MSC Programmes and Special Measures. The numbers involved are shown in Fig.1. Rather than discuss these in more detail here, it might be useful to conclude with some observations about the way ahead. A number of clear policy development priorities have emerged over the recent period:

a) A major objective for the next few years will be the consolidation of the Youth Training Scheme. In particular the emphasis will be on ensuring that the scheme is work-based, on encouraging employers to

58 Will the Future Work?

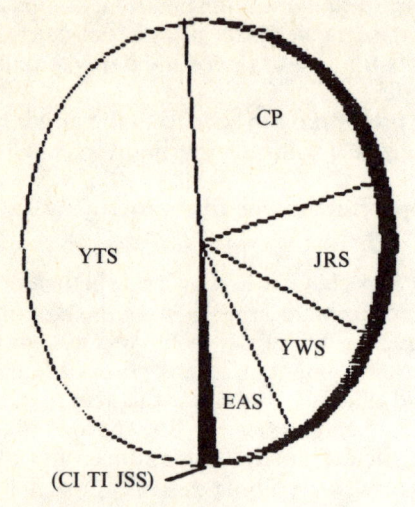

FIGURE 1: NUMBER OF PEOPLE COVERED BY SPECIAL EMPLOYMENT AND TRAINING MEASURES IN GREAT BRITAIN AT THE END OF APRIL 1985

(CI)	Community Industry	8,000
(CP)	Community Programme	133,000
(EAS)	Enterprise Allowance Scheme	43,000
(JRS)	Job Release Scheme	67,000
(JSS)	Job Splitting Scheme	240
(TI)	Training in Industry	1,500
(YWS)	Young Workers Scheme	58,000
(YTS)	Youth Training Scheme	292,000

Total: 602,740

The Department of Employment estimates that the direct effect of these measures on the official unemployment (claimants) count at the end of April was a reduction in the count of 445,000.

bring more of their 16 year-old employees into the scheme, and in ensuring the quality of individual schemes and the training offered.

b) A second major objective will be to carry through the Adult Training Strategy by efforts to change attitudes, enhance provision and remodel MSC's own directly provided services. Proposals for pilot projects under the new Strategy are at present being implemented; it is intended that the range of pilot projects will cover both programmes of job-related training and help for the unemployed.

c) Third, it is the Commission's intention to continue to encourage the modernization of training arrangements for both adults and young people. This objective is an integral element of the Commission's

overall strategy as the development of an accepted system of training to standards will open the way to access to appropriate training and hence to jobs by individuals throughout the course of their working lives.
d) Within the Employment Service the focus will remain on a continuing search for greater efficiency in the provision and development of current labour market services. One particularly important aspect is developing the "gateway" function of the job centres, which serves to open up the full range of MSC services, particularly on the training side, to unemployed and employed persons alike.
e) Also within employment services there are important questions to be addressed on help for particularly disadvantaged groups. The increasing prominence of long-term unemployment raises questions of whether access to training might be provided along with the temporary work provided on the Community Programme. The Commission is currently considering this and initial indications are that ministers are keen to add a sound training dimension to the Programme. For disabled people, Commission staff try, as far as possible, to encourage the integration of the disabled into the labour market as a whole, whereas disabled people who have special employment needs will be given access to an *improved* specialist service.

I should add a word of caution. The programme for further action which I have outlined attempts to identify the lines on which national effort must go forward, particularly in the field of training for jobs. However, much remains to be done and there will be many obstacles to progress in the coming period. It will be necessary and important for MSC's programmes to continue to be developed and adjusted as experience and events dictate. To this end considerable emphasis is being put on the monitoring and evaluation of MSC's various programmes.

More importantly, however, the responsibility for the success of these programmes must go far beyond the Commission itself to rest with all those involved at specific practical levels—with employers, with the education authorities and other training providers and with the trade unions and the labour force more generally. Given the rapid rate at which the economy is developing and restructuring there seems a very obvious need for all of these groups to have closer and better communications with each other in order to allow better identification of the changing requirements of industry and the labour force and to speed up and improve the response of the MSC and the providers of other training and employment services.

International Perspectives: the European Community

MARC LENDERS

The European Ecumenical Commission for Church and Society (EECCS) recently adopted a text dealing with what has become the main social issue within the European Community: the unemployment of an increasing number of men and women, and of young people in particular. According to EEC statistics, the 13-million mark has been passed. Among these 13 million, 40 per cent are young people under the age of 25. Moreover there has been a sharp increase in long-term unemployment in the last few years.

In the face of this reality, it has to be admitted that until now, the various and sometimes divergent measures taken by the member states have not been sufficient to stop the rising curve of unemployment. The European Community now pays the heavy toll of a lack of voluntary social policy at community level taking into account the increasing interdependence of the various national economies. The golden sixties have masked the need for a greater understanding between the various social policies within the European Community. It is hard to imagine how, given the current crisis which automatically brings about introspection, that social solidarity at Community level could see the light of day.

The crisis has a double effect: it creates a division between those who are rejected by the labour market and those who have jobs but fear losing them; it could in the long term mean a resurgence of nationalistic tendencies, each country trying to make others bear the weight of unemployment. Some are not far from thinking that unless we change course, we will end up with a Latin-Americanization of our societies, the only difference being that these countries are young and rich, and possess raw materials, whereas our countries are aging and have few natural resources. Taking up the imagery used in a report on unemployment submitted to the European Parliament, the European Community could be compared to a rich old lady living on her private income and selling her jewels. The "no-future" of punks is another aspect of the tragedy of unemployment and reinforces the validity of this image. Indeed the current unemployment situation is characterized by a lack of prospects and of solidarity. Surveys conducted nowadays on how unemployment was experienced in the 30s confirm these characteristics *a contrario*. In the 30s there was hope for change and greater solidarity at the local level. Today, the unemployed hide and are kept hidden. They know that in many cases the job they had will not turn up again because it will have ceased to exist.

Indeed, in order to assess the extent of the unemployment problem, the overwhelming changes brought about by the technological developments have to be taken into account. This technological evolution poses the countries of the European Community a big problem. Rejecting technological change means even greater dependence on political and economic leaders in this field. Accepting it blindly means taking the risk of entering a dualistic society and sacrificing what has characterized the Community member states, i.e. the search for a balance between the rights of the individual and social responsibility. The only way out of the dilemma is, in my opinion, to reject the determinism of technological evolution and to regain control of its development. Unfortunately, in comparison with the economic giants bringing about these technological changes, national powers seem very weak and helpless. Again we face the idea of an authority which would be geographically broad enough in its field of application and disciplined enough to lead to this essential recovery.

What has been described so far is merely a summary of the analysis of a situation which, in my opinion, is sufficiently borne out by the facts. We feel that the attached commentary is well-founded. I say "we" because the thoughts of the working group convened by the Ecumenical Commission has led to this commentary, which justifies the invitation made to the churches to undertake action at EEC level independently of actions undertaken at the national level.

What hope of salvation outside the European Community? None; the way *via* the European Community seems inevitable to us because of the interdependence of national economies and the need for a common agreement in the face of regionally grouped political and economic forces operating at the international level. However, although this condition is necessary, it is far from being sufficient. It will only make sense if it is coupled with reflection and action on the nature of work itself, as a prerequisite towards fundamental discussion on the very substance of this European Community.

Unemployment in the European Community in the 80s is not a phenomenon due to poor economic growth, it is also having drastic effects on the economic and social landscape, with repercussions at the political level still to come. It affects the heart of a society which valued work by turning it into an essential aspect of human dignity. It is the sign of a society in crisis whose old values are now obsolete and crumbling away, unable to give birth to new values which could open a possible future for the men and women that constitute it. The future forms of our society will depend largely on the answers given to the problem of unemployment.

It has often been said that the European Community is characterized by its inability to define its goals and aims. Born from a will for reconciliation and from the desire to guarantee better social justice, it has let itself progressively become imprisoned in a labyrinth of regulations, concentrated mainly on economic and commercial realities. It is out of breath.

Persisting and growing unemployment should be viewed in the context of a European Community unable to define its objectives. It also raises the basic question of a society's organization and objectives. All these questions show the need for the churches to enter a debate in which they will have to intervene according to their specific character.

Their starting point in the debate will not consist in economic or political considerations, it will start from a vision of the human person. This will mean, on the one hand, that the human being cannot be reduced to a mere force of production while on the other hand, his/her dignity expresses itself, in a very particular way, in work. The first part of this statement means that when considering the problem of unemployment nowadays, one should not lose sight of the aspect of the quality of work. Of course, any type of work includes an element of productivity, but the aspects of creativity and responsibility and of one's environment (working place, society, nature) should also be integrated in all kinds of work. The second part of the statement evokes the irreplaceable function of work in maintaining the human person's dignity.

Insofar as our society places an excessive value on paid work at the expense of other forms of work, any job loss is experienced as an amputation, a lessening of one's value. All surveys conducted on the subject show this to be the existential character of unemployment.

This means that if the churches want to base their efforts on how unemployment is experienced, they should first reject the determinist ideology surrounding these social and economic changes. They should recall to the authorities and the responsible actors that they should reject what is more and more frequently presented as a totally inevitable situation. It is therefore necessary to control the process and to ensure the participation of those directly concerned by the changes taking place.

The churches, whose task it is to announce the advent of the kingdom of God, should proclaim, in the face of current evidence to the contrary, a future which could be possible for men and women and for the young whom our society condemns to inactivity and for those who are left by the wayside because they no longer meet productivity criteria.

The crisis we are going through forces us to choose between the constraints of an economic world where competitiveness reigns and to which the European Community is subjected because of its immediate international context (USA/Japan), and the requirements of an evangelical world where sharing and solidarity between men and women are stressed. At stake in the debate is a challenge calling for an operational response in view of the context and corresponding to the criteria which guide the churches' efforts. It is not a matter of opposing "economism" to "evangelism"; otherwise the debate would come to a sudden end. Moreover, an operational response does not mean the elaboration of a programme for society. It is a matter of finding orientations which could be applied in the immediate term, reasons for living for today and tomorrow.

The Ecumenical Commission's document on "Unemployment and the Future of Work" draws the conclusions of a process under way within the national churches of western Europe; the replacement of the church-state relationship by a church-society relationship. This substitution signals the break-up of centres of power and the desire of the churches to consolidate their opinions on issues arising from the organization of urban life. The church-state dyarchy characterized by a permanent pursuit of a balance between two forms of power has become eroded by the questions of the nation-state and its destructive effects in Europe and in the world, and by the redistribution and transnationalization of economic powers. Parallel to this, as the churches came out of the Constantinian era, they were forced, sometimes willingly, sometimes reluctantly, to abandon their claims to exert power over the organization of civil life. The European Community is too vague an entity to allow a European "nationalism" to replace the nationalisms of the nation-states. Scepticism towards the European Community cannot be based on this line of reasoning which goes against the facts. On the other hand, the existence of the European Community reveals the internationalization taking place within our society. If nation-states exist, there is also a society in western Europe with common characteristics.

In this sense, the vagueness and imprecision of the contours could be interpreted positively. Indeed, this transitory situation allows the churches to be responsible in the face of social problems such as unemployment, by taking the international dimension and the radical character of the problems into account. When analyzing the actors who possess powers of decision or influence, we can observe that, except for the churches, there are few who take the international dimension and the global vision of the problem into account.

Often we look for short-term solutions in the national context. Thus it comes as no surprise that the solutions implemented appear as stopgap measures and that public opinion loses confidence in the face of such inability to solve problems.

Given these facts, the churches can, on the basis of their particular vocation, take upon themselves this *international dimension* which is in accordance with the universalism they proclaim, provided that this universalism is neither abstract nor theoretical. Universalism means learning to look beyond the immediate borders making concern visible for the "distant neighbour". Visser 't Hooft was aware that this chance was already lost by the church—when national socialism and fascism came to power—to find forms of transnational coresponsibility. For this same reason he welcomed the establishment of international institutions as a way and means to enhance transnational corporations which the churches ought to take seriously by monitoring them.

The churches can also contribute to placing the questions which have arisen in their *proper perspective* by taking *all the various aspects* of a problem into account. In the case of unemployment, the need for such an approach has been demonstrated. A compartmentalized approach of the issue can only provide incomplete solutions which, in the long run, prove to be inefficient.

In view of the short-term character of the solutions considered today, imposed by both the need to deal with the most urgent things first and by electoral considerations, the churches should bear in mind the need to take the *long-term perspective* into account in their reflections and in the modes of implementation envisaged. What is needed is a definition of the objectives which are likely to gain support and mobilization, since without these, no project can really take shape.

Because the churches are locally implanted and reach a larger public than the political or social machineries in place, they can be *places of access to social problems*. Adequate, flexible structures at parish-level offer a wide range of possible local and concrete action.

These *notae ecclesiarum* which could serve as a definition of the role of the ecclesiastical community vis-à-vis the secular community in the context of an internationalization of social issues, may be spelled out in a more concrete way as far as the issue of unemployment is concerned.

The universal dimension: What does "distant neighbour" mean in the context of looking for a solution to the problem of unemployment? Repercussions on the third world, on poorer regions. Sharing among those who are employed and those who are not.

The holistic approach of the problem: A need to understand that the search for a solution to unemployment means recognizing its environment (urban and rural areas, state of economic and social distintegration) as well as need for an in-depth reflection on the meaning of work.

The notion of hope The refusal to consider technological evolution as a blind fatality which destroys—without alternative—entire fields of

economic activities in the various professional sectors (in the services sector, office automation; in industry, automation; in agriculture, mechanization). The need to control these developments. In order to do this it is necessary to:
1) work out possible future scenarios; in particular, it would be necessary for the economic paradigms to include variables such as ecological cost as well as the impact on developing countries;
2) introduce the long-term aspect into decision-making;
3) orientate development on the basis of a democratic debate focusing on the objectives and means to achieve them.

The elaboration of a teaching process and of action models at the level of *local churches*: the universal dimension, the holistic approach and an open attitude towards the future may all be found in concrete form at the local level, in a teaching process intended for church members, by setting up micro-projects intended to show solidarity with individuals experiencing unemployment.

Given the fact that our churches are often characterized as being inward-looking, such a demand will no doubt seem unrealistic. Ernst Bloch makes a distinction between day dreams and night dreams. The latter refer to the past while day dreams concern the future.

The unemployment crisis which is affecting millions of individuals and whose end no one dares predict, is progressively paralyzing a society of over 250 million people. Yet it has, if it wants to, the resources and potential necessary to combat unemployment.

The precondition for a change of the situation is to dare to have day dreams and to try to make them come true.

As witnesses to the gospel proclaiming the kingdom of God, the churches have a special responsibility to proclaim the right to believe in a "somewhere else" in a world struggling beneath a mass of facts and figures; with the means entrusted to them, they have the duty to transpose the "dream" into real everyday life.

International Perspectives: Malaysia's Electronics Industry

STEPHEN MAXWELL

Some of the most dramatic employment-creating effects of the microelectronics revolution are to be seen in the rapidly-industrializing countries of South East Asia. Malaysia is a good example. The most spectacular success of Malaysia's policy of encouraging export-oriented industrialization from 1970 has undoubtedly been the electronics industry. The industry was introduced to Malaysia in 1967 when two Japanese companies, Matsushita and Toshiba, began to assemble television receivers for the domestic market. But with an annual output of only US$2.4m. in 1967 Malaysia hardly figured in the same league as Taiwan with production worth US$38.6m., Hong Kong with its US$108.9m. or even Singapore with its US$18.5m.

The major expansion of the Malaysian electronics industry came in the early 1970s. It differed from the early phase of electronics development in the leading Asian electronics producers by being firmly biased towards the production of components rather than consumer goods. By the mid-1970s many of the world's leading electronics companies were established in Malaysia, with semi-conductor firms particularly well represented—Hewlett-Packard, Hitachi, Motorola, National Semiconductor, Intel, Litronix, Mostek, Advanced Micro Devices, Nippon Electric, Texas Instruments. By 1980 over 80 per cent of Malaysia's electronics production consisted of components, compared to 60 per cent for Singapore and 50 per cent or less for South Korea, Taiwan and Hong Kong. By the end of the 1970s Malaysia had established itself as the largest exporter of semi-conductor devices in Asia, ahead of Singapore and Japan.

The attraction of the electronics industry to Malaysia's economic planners was that it was a labour-intensive industry which held out the promise of thousands of new jobs to a country embarking on a major piece of social engineering. The rapid build-up of employment between 1972 and 1974 vindicated the planners' judgment. But by the mid-1970s the most dramatic period of growth in the electronics components industry was over. After the 1974–75 recession when Malaysia lost 6,000 electronics jobs the flow of new jobs never reached its earlier level. Automation of binding and testing—two of the most labour-intensive stages in semi-conductor production—began to be introduced. Overseas employment of the United States semi-conductor firms, which had grown from 40,000 in 1969 to 85,000 in 1974, grew by only 4,000 in the next four years. In the later 1970s other Asian countries offering even cheaper labour than Malaysia—notably the Philippines, but also Sri Lanka, Thailand and followed by India and the People's Republic of China—began to compete for new electronics investment. National Semiconductor for example, which had opened a plant in Malaysia in 1972, opened another in the Philippines in 1976 where it was followed three years later by Motorola which had also opened in Malaysia in 1972.

It was in response to this slowing of the rate of growth of new electronics jobs rather than as part of a long-term strategy for the development of a Malaysian controlled electronics industry, that Malaysian politicians and planners began to talk of the need to upgrade the technological content of the Malaysian electronics industry. There has continued to be more talk than action. There is provision within the guidelines of Malaysian development policy to direct state aid and other development privileges towards new investment promising higher technology and a higher proportion of management, technical and supervisory staff. But Malaysia has not evolved a strategy remotely comparable to Singapore's strategy for upgrading the technological content of its industry. In the absence of a strategy the statements of ministers have not always been consistent. When the minister for trade and industry officially opened an electronics training centre built by the United States company Mostek in Kelantan state in 1983, he looked forward to the emergence of an "integrated electronics industry producing 100 per cent made in Malaysia products". But in the same month the Malaysian prime minister on a visit to South Korea was reported as urging South Korean businessmen to invest in labour-intensive, low-technology assembly operations in Malaysia.

The state government of Penang, Malaysia's own Silicon Valley, continually emphasizes the need to replace its present labour-intensive operations with high-tech capital intensive operations. And it can point to examples in its local electronics industry. In 1984, National Semiconductor opened a new technologically sophisticated testing building. Atlas Industries, a Hong Kong based company, has set up a new factory to manufacture a range of electronic products including computer drives and digital magnetic eraser heads.

Perhaps the state's favourite example is the United States company Advanced Micro-Devices. AMD started in Penang in the Bayan Lepas Free Trade Zone in 1972 employing some 75 workers on the classic labour intensive semi-conductor operations. By 1983 AMD had automated most of the labour-intensive stages—such as lead bonding, die attachment and saw operations—while increasing its labour force to 2,800. At a ceremony in August 1984 to mark the opening of a new AMD automatic testing facility the chief minister of Penang state, Dr Lim Chong Eu, congratulated AMD for its "exemplary efforts" at transferring technology to Malaysia, as demonstrated by the fact that 438 of the firm's employees were training in various institutions of higher studies in Malaysia and abroad. But overall in Bayan Lepas only 17.2 per cent of the labour force had received in-house training with a further 3.5 per cent being sponsored for external courses of one sort or another. The extent of Malaysia's continuing technological dependence in electronics is revealed in the occupational wage survey conducted by the ministry of labour:

SKILLS PROFILE OF THE ELECTRONICS LABOUR FORCE IN MALAYSIA

	1974 %	*1977* %	*1980* %	*1983* %
Professional and technical	0.6	0.6	0.7	0.6
Administrative and managerial	0.7	0.6	0.7	0.5
Clerical	3.7	4.2	3.5	3.3
Service	—	0.3	0.4	0.4
Production workers				
skilled	11.5	13.8	12.9	12.1
unskilled	83.6	80.5	81.9	83.1

The figures show that over the life-time of the electronics industry in Malaysia there has been no upgrading of the skill level of the work-force.

Official Malaysian claims of "high-tech" status for the Malaysian electronics industry have to be treated with care. Semi-conductor production embodies high levels of technology, increasingly so as automation is introduced. But the technology is enclosed in the production technology and cannot easily be transferred to the production workers. Lacking a technological tradition of its own or a strong research base Malaysia appears to be firmly caught in the trap of "technology dependence".

In the semi-conductor industry itself the application of electronics based automation to the assembly stages of production has reduced the attractions of low-labour cost locations in the third world in favour of developed country locations like Scotland and the United States. But third world countries will continue to attract investment in electronics assembly, offering work-forces which are not only lower paid but willing to work more flexibly and intensively in poorer working conditions with fewer overheads, so maximizing the return on the investment cost of the new automated processes.

Applied to other areas of manufacturing, electronics-based automation will reduce but not eliminate the attractions of third world locations. Perhaps the greatest challenge for third world countries lies in applying electronics to the design of new products and the design and control of complete production and distribution systems, rather than to sub-processes such as assembly. Third world countries will face a number of obstacles in seeking to utilize the new technologies, including shortages of skill (at systems management level rather than operator level), distance from the servicing facilities of the suppliers of the new technologies, and, of course, the foreign currency costs of purchasing the technologies. While in theory multinational companies as the main purchasers of the new electronic technologies might regard the systems gains of operating with flexible third world labour forces as counterbalancing these disadvantages, the growth of protectionism in developed countries—partly in response to the labour displacing effects of the diffusion of new technologies there—creates an additional obstacle to the transfer of expensive technologies to third world locations. The available evidence suggests that the introduction of the new technologies is widening the technological gap in manufacturing between developed and developing countries to penetrate developed country markets.

The challenge which the electronics revolution presents to the developing nations is not limited to manufacturing. Perhaps the most crucial impact of electronics will be in the new information industries.

The convergence of electronic information processing, data banks and telecommunication systems into a single information network is a development of fundamental importance to third world development prospects. The global information network which has been created is a monopoly of developed countries, substantially of United States multinational companies. While the third world has 78 per cent of the world's population, generates 20 per cent of world trade and is responsible for 12–13 per cent of the world's industrial output, it has only 7 per cent of the world's telephones, 6 per cent of computers, 3 per cent of research and development expenditure and 5 per cent of science and technology publications.

In this network the developing country has two roles—as a supplier of raw data on everything from mineral resources and crop forecasts to market surveys, government expenditure programmes and credit ratings, and as a recipient of processed information and other media products. But while it supplies much of the information unpaid, even as with satellite surveillance of crop prospects, unwittingly, it has to pay for most of the processed information and media products it takes from the global network.

The economic issues raised by the "electronics revolution" emerged as an issue in North-South political relations at the 1982 meetings of GATT (General Agreement on Tariffs and Trade), when the United States moved to pre-empt third world proposals to control the trade in services by putting the liberalization of services' trade on the agenda as bargaining counter to third world demands for the liberalization of trade in manufactures.

The implications of the developed country control of the global information network spread beyond economics to the cultural and political. The cultural issue has surfaced in calls sponsored by UNESCO for a New World Information Order strengthening national communications networks, particularly in the flow of information, and ideas and cultural values from North to South.

For a third world electronics producer like Malaysia, it is a cruel irony—it supplies the cheap labour to make the electronic components which when put to work in manufacturing and the new information industries confirm its dependence and increase its vulnerability to exploitation.

PART III

An Alternative Work Ethic?

Employment and the Theology of Work

DAVID BLEAKLEY

As a former engineer with long involvement in church and trade union matters, I want to look beyond our immediate industrial tensions, considering in particular what sort of Christian response might be offered to the wider industrial revolution in which we are involved. I take as a guideline a quotation from President Kenneth Kaunda:

> When Man learns, by bitter experience, if in no other way, that the only hope for the peace and happiness of the world is to give social, political and economic expression to love for others, we shall be in the presence not of the Kingdom of Man, but of the Kingdom of God.

Those are wise words, directing us to the meaning of mission, and they are particularly apt for Christians seeking to give direction to the rapid social and economic transformation which is a distinguishing feature of our time. Particularly for whole communities the change in life-style has become an awesome experience. Increasingly we are aware that we are not in just another recession—we are at the end of an era. Samuel Beckett's words sum it up for many: "We are between a death and a difficult birth."

In these circumstances I can well understand the feelings of the thousands of men and women with whom I served my shipyard apprenticeship—workers who have been scattered by technological changes which they hardly understand and for which they have been ill-prepared. That Belfast shipyard once employed 30,000 men and women—now there are 5,000.

Some of the fear seeping into those who feel threatened by new technology was expressed at a recent British trade union conference when an emotional standing ovation was given to a steelman from northern England who shared his plight with delegates. It was the epitaph of a hardworking man of 54 who had worked in the industry for 38 years. He was telling of the end of his job: "When I finish I will go the same way as other out-of-work steel workers. I will do nothing till I die."

Those are desperate and lonely words, yet that is the way many of those caught up in today's industrial shake-out perceive their plight. And the worldwide confrontations in the mines, transport and other older industries reflect this same desperation—we are seeing the bewilderment of ordinary men and women who have been persuaded that the only life they know is about to vanish. They feel threatened, and the threat is as much spiritual as it is economic.

In all this, the church has a key role to play. Reaching out as it does to every part of society, it can help men and women to free themselves from partisan attitudes which are obsolescent in today's circumstances; and it must be prepared to act as responding guide, helping its people to play a positive participatory role in the reshaping of the social and economic order.

Many years ago Archbishop William Temple pointed the way when he advised the church to not be afraid in articulating the Christian social demand—provided we were always prepared to encourage our people to discover its application for themselves.

Yet it has not been easy for Christians, particularly the laity, to obtain guidance from church leadership on the great social issues of the ages—and especially on questions to do with industrial relations generally and work in particular.

Nor for most people do the scriptures provide much help. Though the Old Testament is vastly more informed on work relationships than the Gospels, it is not easy to base a modern Christian approach to the problems of work on what has been called "inconclusive fragmentariness".

Unfortunately the church has come late in the day to a fuller appreciation of the importance of work in people's lives; and in a fast-changing industrial scene the catching-up process is not easy. Indeed, many theological colleges have failed to grasp the importance of upgrading industrial studies for their students. Worse still, as one noted Roman Catholic theologian has observed: "The modern theology of work attempts to give meaning to work precisely at a time when it appears to have become meaningless through industrialization."

The fact of the matter is that "work" as a topic for study was not high on the theological agenda of the Christian fathers—for the most part, it was an accepted way of life. Certainly, it was not a subject which church councils would have sat down to discuss as a major item on the agenda. In fact, the church did not become conscious about industrial problems until well into the Industrial Revolution. Reflections on the subject arose mainly in reaction to the issues raised by this Revolution— problems to do with the factory system, methods of production, hours and conditions of labour, terms of employment, fluctuations in employment levels, trade unions, and so on.

There is still much wisdom in a comment made nearly a quarter of a century ago:

> It may be suggested that we will not find a satisfactory Christian theology of work ready made for us in the past, and that the twentieth century has to work out its own situations in the light of twentieth century conditions, even though what men have thought about work in the past may help us in some degree to avoid their errors and profit from their wisdom.[1]

However, it is also fair to note that it is not only the church which has been at fault in failing to grasp the significance of work in human lives. As E.F. Schumacher underlined in his own pioneer study *Good Work*, for the most part, we look in vain for theories of work in academic textbooks on economics, sociology, politics and related subjects:

> The question of what work does to the worker is hardly ever asked, not to mention the question of whether the real task might not be to adapt the work to the needs of the worker rather than to demand that the worker adapt himself to the needs of the work...[2]

And accordingly, when the church *has* spoken out, the main thrust has been to offer inspirational lectures on the dignity of labour, thus providing justification for the aims and practices of the champions of the industrial system. Unfortunately it was a far from balanced contribution; the views of those who actually performed the labour and who were at the "sharp end" of the industrial process were in the main ignored.

And this remains one of the great credibility problems facing the church when it seeks to give leadership to the working class—it is one thing to analyse the problems of unemployment, but it is quite another to confront this problem as a personal terminal illness, affecting the divinely ordinary things of life.

All too often the church has buried itself in a theology of the cloister instead of embracing a theology of the market place. How different the future might have been if the intellectual giants of the Christian faith in the nineteenth century had concentrated on the issues which tormented the mass of their fellow citizens. As an example, the Church of England was racked with fierce doctrinal debates which, though intellectually exciting to those who lived on the banks of Oxford, seemed distinctly remote from a life that was endured on the seedier stretches of the Thames in London. Thus not for the first time the church establishment made the error of failing to recognize that the command "Christ is Lord" embraces all life. This point was not lost on its working class flock; it became a powerful factor in emptying the pews of inner-city churches.

Yet, the Industrial Revolution brought deeply spiritual problems to plague those involved in the productive process. High on the list was what Schumacher called the "folklore of incentives which magnifies individual egotism in direct opposition to the teaching of the Gospel". In fact, the dominant processes of industrial society have alienated neighbour from neighbour, emphasizing a material relationship and demanding a pointless action described well by one poet as "the opium of the individual". In the face of such challenges the proletariat were left to fend for themselves.

Hence we inherit what Roger Clarke has identified as something which goes much deeper than merely economic matters:

> What I see in the present situation constitutes a fracture of fellowship, the recreation and perpetuation of an underclass in the midst of otherwise comparative affluence.[3]

But we should not be trapped by frameworks which ignore the Spirit, we can break the spell and enter into the exploration for which we were created. New technology, revealed and accepted as God's latest gift, can make the transformation possible. In present circumstances, and whatever the pace and action of government and other secular institutions, the church must be prepared to act as a responding community, helping society to achieve a sense of direction which will underline the oneness of humanity as we shape, and are shaped by, a new social and economic order.

Nor are Christians entirely unprepared for the transformation struggle. Even at the height of Britain's Industrial Revolution there were some who protested at the indifference of the church to social reform. F.D. Maurice, for example, warned "that while religious men are disputing, the great body of Englishmen is becoming indifferent to us all and smiles grimly and contemptuously at our controversies". Then, too, many of those who felt excluded by the established church found an alternative in Methodism, forging lasting links between the Labour movement and non-conformity.

More recently the British Council of Churches has been a "new frontiers" base, and talented communicators like William Temple, Donald Soper, Colin Morris, John V. Taylor and Trevor Huddleston have used their gifts to reach out to a radical constituency of Christian support. More notably David Sheppard, with his "bias to the poor", has been identified with a new generation of social reformers.

In our post-war world, particularly with the growing emergence of third world Christian communities (all supported by the World Council of Churches), "awareness" has become one of the great Christian themes, with a searching range of questions to express the new emphasis. For example, questions like: Why have the churches in the Western and Eastern blocs been so reluctant to challenge the social status quo? Why do we limit the Lordship of Christ? How do we apply Christian principles to international trade or to the exploitation of defenceless primary producers? And how does the church respond to strife-torn industrial societies and to men and women who feel threatened by new technology?

The urgency of these appeals is a powerful confirmation that we have reached a watershed in human history, and that we are concluding an era calling for many "endings" and many "new beginnings", dealing with work relationships, productive processes and the entire system of distribution and exchange. Inevitably such a convergence exerts a relentless pressure on existing institutions, both national and international, producing contradictions which must be resolved if chaos is to be avoided.

Langdon Gilkey, Lesslie Newbigin, Edward Scott and a wide range of modern Christian prophets have from their own perspectives noted the historical transformation which is afoot. But equally significant, there is among the mass of people today a "collective unconsciousness" that a process of social and industrial change has started from which, in its broad outline, there is no turning back.

The millions caught up in this revolution of our time constitute a silent majority who must be heard. Like the steel workers who see redundancy as marking the end of their working lives. Or like the youngster at a drop-in-centre for unemployed who once expressed: "I've done nothing since I left school three years ago. What will I do if I *never* get a job? Sometimes lying in bed at night, I come out in a cold sweat when I think of that."

These are widespread, desperate, lonely fears; and it is central to the modern mission of the church to share the "cold sweat" of that youngster. This "sharing" will require a recognition that the problems of our post-industrial society are primarily moral and spiritual, a result of the values of our age. Earthly disciplines dealing with cost-effectiveness and the like certainly have their place, but only when the "simple arithmetic" which they represent gives pride of place to a "higher calculus" which is essential for all who consider the human condition.

In seeking to influence the debate about ways and means which must take place as we go through this difficult period of social and economic change, the church is suitably placed to influence the outcome. More than any other group in society, Christians must be aware that the status quo is not necessarily part of the Divine Order of things and that no social order can demand a writ of immortality. More importantly, the prophetic role of the churches requires that they be prepared to draw attention to social writs which have run their course.

The World Council of Churches at Vancouver, 1983, heard something of this when Moderator Archbishop Ted Scott warned against the dangers of "cultural captivity" and disclaimed allegiance to today's two competing ideologies—capitalism and communism. He also pointed to great similarities in these two systems, in particular their stress on materialism and their concern for persons as units of production and consumption.

Neither of these ideologies was seen as adequately responding to the challenges which confront us. Both were on the defensive and involved in confrontations which threaten all of human life. Moderator Scott left us with this challenge: "If churches are to break out of their cultural captivity and avoid the ever-present danger of substituting a limited emphasis on individual piety for the proclamation of the sovereignty of God, they must again discover a transcendent loyalty which is strong enough to enable them 'to be in the world but not of it'."

So, in a delicate balance, we are recommended to look beyond both systems for salvation—the greed of capitalism and the coercion of communism are equally deficient. And, of course, whatever the national setting there is an international context to such challenges. However, there is clear evidence that the fact of our international interdependence has sunk home—in all nation states, both sides of industry have a tendency to seek remedies which in effect mean exporting unemployment. How we respond as nations to this situation will tell us much about the kind of people we are. Can the churches give a lead which will ensure that a recognition of our God-created oneness permeates social and economic thinking at national and international level?

Poverty anywhere threatens the prosperity of all, but we need not only economic solutions; we need ideas to inspire them. Here, if ever, is an area for Christian action. To transform society—to get from "here to there"—remains the problem. Like Langdon Gilkey we cannot see clearly what is afoot and we are only too aware of our uncertainties.

There is also truth in the warning of Daniel Bell who, writing several years ago, warned us that "to be hypnotized by such dangers is little less than frivolous". There is a powerful message to be probed in his reminder that no social or economic order has "a writ of immortality"; that the consumer-oriented free enterprise society no longer satisfies as it once did; that it will have to change so that a free society might still survive; and that we are now moving to a sharing ethic, without that community being as yet defined.[4]

And that precisely is the problem facing modern industrial society; as we carry on within our contemporary industrial framework on which so many depend, we have at the same time to make fundamental changes in order to pave the way for the transformation that must take place. As so often is the case in real life, we have to write a new score while at the same time we play the only music we know. Lewis Mumford's problem of "dynamic equilibrium" remains with us.

What sort of specific challenges confront Christians in today's conditions of rapid and industrial change? Each of us will speak from out of our particular situation, but there are many general social and economic contradictions which must trouble the Christian conscience, which represent the lack of love which Kenneth Kaunda identified in our earlier quotation, and which challenge the Pauline doctrine that we are members one of another.

The contradiction represented by unemployment is such a challenge. The injustice and folly of modern unemployment is apparent to the millions who have been caught up in the process. What is happening is seen as unjust because the burden instead of being shared by the whole community is thrust on the shoulders of those least able to bear it; and the process is seen as a folly when the cost of unemployment benefit is computed. In such contradictions the modern market economy loses its credibility, both morally and financially.

For the unemployed the reality is often that of being trapped in a social welfare system based on out-of-date assumptions—like that which assumes that unemployment will be no more than a year in duration; or that which regards the so-called "black economy" as totally reprehensible. Should not Christians be calling for welfare strategies which express a compassion appropriate to a post-industrial society? Or at another level, how far does "bearing one another's burdens" call for radical advances in job sharing schemes and an extension to manual workers of the more flexible and comprehensive conditions applicable in professional occupations (sabbaticals, paid educational leave and so on).

Other contradictions abound. Like the one which suggests that there is a surplus of teachers—all at a time when millions of children throughout the world struggle to learn in over-full classes and when we are confidently assured that the best schools are normally those with a favourable teacher/pupil ratio. Equally disturbing is the suggestion that we are beginning to produce a surplus of doctors in a world full of mental and physical suffering. Or, we hear about the twilight of traditional labour when all around great areas of vital work remain unattended—housing, the environment, the caring services are just a few areas which come to mind.

Quite simply, there is no shortage of work in our far-from-perfect world. The fact of the matter is that even at this point in human affairs, unemployment bears little relationship to the amount of work that needs to be done. The problems of adjusting to this reality are considerable, but are less than the social tensions which will accompany a policy of neglect. What is required is a shift away from materialistic notions which measure profitability basically in terms of a financial calculation. We need a new and truer measurement of the value of work—one which will take us beyond equating work only with a job, a paid position supplied by the market.

By such a standard it will be a long time before we catch up with the arrears of undone work and create the quality of life we most desire within our lifetime. And properly used, God's gift of new technology can provide the basis for the emancipation of work—transforming much of it from drudgery into a delight.

But what if during the pass-over period from one industrial society to another there remain groups for whom no wage-work is available? Here comes the real test for the principle of familyhood. Unless we are compassionate we run the risk of creating a society of serfs and princelings. The dilemma is vividly put by Wassily Leontief, Nobel prize winner in economics, in a borrowing from the Genesis story:

> Adam and Eve enjoyed, before they were expelled from Paradise, a high standard of living without working. After their expulsion they and their successors were condemned to eke out a miserable existence, working from dawn to dusk. The history of technical progress over the past two hundred years is essentially the story of the human species working its way slowly and steadily back into Paradise.
>
> What would happen, however, if we suddenly found ourselves in Paradise? Well, with all goods and services provided without work, no one would be gainfully employed. And being unemployed means receiving no wages.
>
> As a result, until appropriate new incomes policies were formulated to fit the changed technical conditions, everyone would starve in Paradise.[5]

The contradiction is indeed bizarre, yet for many it could, and has, become a threatening possibility. But society can and must make choices. If we choose a covenant between man and machine based on the affirmation that men and women are God's creation, uniquely created in one human family for a divine purpose, then all will be well. But if mammon becomes the centre of our moral gravity, the nightmares of Huxley and Orwell will become our plight.

The challenge is a spiritual and moral one. If we are to make a truly national journey of social and industrial transformation we cannot make fish of one and flesh of another. Some form of social wage will become the symbol of our willingness to share on the journey. There is nothing very revolutionary in the notion of people having money for "doing nothing" in terms of wage work. Those with inherited wealth have long enjoyed the experience, and most of us at some period in life have had benefit from scholarships or social security without going to pieces. Indeed, as Bertrand Russell once reminded us, "without a leisure class mankind would never have emerged from barbarism".[6]

Here, of course, we run full tilt into what Max Weber called "the spirit of capitalism"—a Protestant work ethic making theologically respectable the drive to make money and to create a social and economic system built on competitive relationships. That ethic has become profoundly counterproductive in today's social setting. R.H. Tawney in a magnificent flourish put it well: "Baptised in the bracing if icy waters of Calvinist theology, the business of life, once regarded as perilous to the soul, acquired a new sanctity. Labour is not merely an economic means; it is a spiritual end".[7]

So, the idea of economic progress as an end to be consciously sought found authority in the identification of labour and enterprise with the service of God. Even today, the ghosts of Luther, Calvin, Adam Smith and Samuel Smiles still haunt us. Major political, industrial and cultural institutions are permeated with the work ethic and schools throughout the world prepare young people for a world which will not be there when they seek to enter it. Again, our hopes for the future rest on a battery of assumptions whose base is manifestly being eroded.

The church has a major responsibility to search for an ethic *for living* which will replace the inherited ethic of working *to make a living*. This involves asking fundamental questions about the nature and meaning of work. Questions like: What is work? Do we really need it? Do we actually want to do wage work or is it a case of Hobson's choice? What do we do when there is no wage available? What is the balance between work and leisure? Can we, in fact, replace an industrial culture that has run its course? Harvey Cox in his *The Secular City* had no doubt:

> Our confusion of human work with a job produced by the market economy proves that our attitudes towards work have not yet been liberated from religious or metaphysical meanings, often held below the level of consciousness.. we still cling to pious attitudes about work, predispositions inherited from a different era. But we shall have to lay aside this idol too. Technopolis demands a new definition of work.[8]

In any case we need not fear the prospect of a non-wage society—it need not be a wasteful condition. On the contrary, as theologian of industry Margaret Kane has pointed out[9] it may release many from degrading toil and allow some people made redundant after years of pointless or monotonous labour to discover themselves for the first time. I cite just one case to make the point—a conversation I had with an unemployed shipyard painter of 58. He had this to say:

> It's nonsense to say you always miss your work when you are paid-off. It all depends on what you have been doing. Over twenty years I worked in the yard as a painter. Day in and day out, nothing but dirt and fumes and noise. Home every night covered in paint and grime. Do you really think I miss all that?

For the first time in my life I can really do all I want to do—get on with my gardening and win prizes at the local club with my roses. And I've got more time to give to the wife and the grand-children. Time doesn't hang on my hands—there's the trade union, the working for Meals on Wheels and help at the local church.

A truly involved person—the inadequacy of the term "unemployed" becomes obvious when measured against such as he. The experience should put us on our guard against shallow applications of the phrase "dignity of labour": we need to remember that a good deal of modern employment is "junk" work, destructive and degrading. Too often human beings are diminished by the demands of the labour market.

Not all will cope with a non-wage work situation such as our shipyard example, but that painter is one of today's "pathfinders"—people of many cultures and many countries who have an instinctive vision of the transition through which we are passing and who devote their time and talents to contributing to its fulfilment. They are "future tense" people—people of the gift economy.

As yet, the pathfinders are in a minority, but they form part of a growing "invisible college" challenging on an international scale the old industrial order. By the lives they are leading these messengers of change begin to question the concept of men and women as mere moneymakers, as cogs in the competitive system, or as an adjunct of new technology. We are learning again that people in community act long before institutionalized theories take note of the need for adaptation. In such situations the status quo is confronted by a "hunch" alternative reflecting a new appreciation of the real-world facts of life—a dialogue of individuals that transcends governments and national boundaries has begun.

In Britain alone it has been calculated that in the voluntary sector (much of it significantly Christian and nicknamed the "white economy") some three million people put in eighteen million hours a week and produce an income for their organizations of £5,000 million. Many of this army of non-waged workers described as "retired" or "young employed"—so "Grey Panthers" and "Young Lions"—combine in creating an alternative economy indicative of things to come. A proliferation of training schemes gives added impetus to the non-wage economy.

In Claude Geffre's phrase: "As often happens in the history of the church, life under the action of the spirit is in advance of thought." Or to put it another way—a new system *is* emerging; the contract may not have been signed, but a deal is being done. Ralf Dahrendorf's faith that individual groups will explore new ways to make the rigid organizations and ideas of yesterday obsolete is being justified.

Employers, unions and government still prefer to think of such developments as temporary or abnormal; but recognized or not, such activities constitute a revision of the work-wage relationship. In time, fuller acceptance of what is now "new" will come and proper accommodation within the social system will be given. Meanwhile, unions and employers should be encouraged by their Christian members to enter more warm-heartedly into the process of change. In particular Christians must seek to avoid the drawing of unfair distinctions between those in traditional employment and those excluded by the market economy.

The thrust towards a post-industrial society is none the less real for being vaguely formulated or resisted by status quo interest groups. Below the level of consciousness there is a stirring of alternatives which comes to the surface long before they are capable of conceptualization. The offering of these "alternatives" is now proceeding as pressures to transform the work ethic build up. Three areas of dogma behind the work ethic are particularly under attack: the glorification of the individual, the suggestion that a person's chief aim is work, and the competitive base for economic activity.

Interestingly, and encouragingly, as disenchantment with the existing status quo spreads, the campaign for revision brings together a political cross-section. So Conservative Edward Heath joins with Socialist Willy Brandt in calling for a new world economic order. And in most European countries there is increasingly, behind the scenes, an informal agenda of concern which links management and labour and party political activists.

A recent book by two former British Labour MPs, Ivor Clemitson and George Rodgers, illustrates the point from the "left". Arguing for a replacement of the work ethic, the writers challenge the traditional attitudes of their own party and call on the trade unions to move beyond out-of-date confines. A powerful case is made for an economic analysis of unemployment which takes into account a redefinition of the work ethic and a consequential questioning of many "sacred cows" on either side of the political divide:

> If the work ethic is not challenged then, inevitably, we are left with only two possible alternatives—full employment and unemployment—and we are prevented from seeing new perspectives and devising new policies based upon those new perspectives... What we are seeking to do is to argue that there are far sounder bases for socialist argument than a narrowly conceived work ethic; bases which are far more appropriate to the age into which we are moving. In short, we need to develop a "life ethic" rather than a "work ethic" and the corresponding concept of "full life" rather than "full employment".[10]

Much of the ferment of ideas about an alternative work ethic is a tribute to the growing reality of interdependence at national and international levels. What is needed now is an application of the principle in social and economic policies which will allow a re-examination of the work ethic and the economic system on which it is dependent.

Application of the principle will require a change of attitude on the part of some of society's strongest institutions. If, for instance, we are to avoid a "two-nation" situation is it possible to continue the market system for profits and wages which both employees and unions favour? To the strongest the spoils? And if the wage work system can no longer ensure a just distribution of work can those who are in control of jobs continue to enjoy a monopoly position? Does the concept of sharing stop at the factory gate? Equally, if a new "mix" between work and leisure is to be achieved how far can the institutions of society be persuaded to change their rules to facilitate the process? And, of fundamental importance, how do we ensure a redistribution of wealth in society sufficient to make possible the fuller life for all implicit in the notion of an interdependent nation? Without such a redistribution "bearing one another's burdens" will have a hollow ring about it.

In any reassessment of the role of work in society, the educationalists will be called upon to play a key part. Can we then achieve a curriculum for our times—not only to do with the "nuts and bolts" of education but with the values we inculcate. In particular, we require a curriculum which will encourage our children, as they grow up in "the global village", to replace the opium of competition with a dynamic which is corporate in scope and centred on cooperation.

I have suggested elsewhere[11] the creation of a ministry of job creation and preservation, with special responsibility for monitoring and considering the human consequences of technical innovation and for giving advice. Such a ministry would provide a focus for public concern and would keep on the parliamentary agenda concerns which if neglected will gravely divide the nation.

No doubt future generations will wonder why we regarded such innovations as anything but natural. But in the meantime, Christians in industry should recognize the paramount need to behave justly to one another during the pass-over period—by bearing one another's burdens we affirm that the earth is the Lord's and the fullness thereof. Indeed, at every level we must proclaim that we are not limited by our resources but by the use to which we put those resources. As a modern prophet has put it: "Till now Man has been up against Nature; from now on he will have to struggle against his own nature".[12]

If we are to win the struggle against mental graven images, we shall need to free ourselves from assumptions that tie us to a fading past. To put it another way: modern technology gives us the escape velocity from the need to accumulate; we are now in a position to explore the nobler reaches of distribution. In the process we shall need to find a new sensitivity which will help us distinguish between the market economy and the gift economy; between the creation of goods and the offering of services; between compulsory labour and choice work. We begin to perceive what one day will be recognized as the Sufficient Society. Above all, in the words of one of our greatest Christian social philosophers:

> What we have to do in the present age is to combine goodness and cleverness; to learn somehow to permeate the vast impersonal world organisations which in this modern world we cannot do without, with the Love of God and of our neighbour. We have to learn to harness the scientific mind in the service of the merciful heart.[13]

In such distinctions lie the new Industrial Revolution of our time.

Two hundred years ago in the first Industrial Revolution we were not so warned or prepared as we are today. Then, for many, the church seemed to make the mistake of being on the side of the *victors* and not the *victims* of the time. Now there is an opportunity to ensure that there are neither victors nor victims—to ensure that in the Christian spirit of familyhood we shall work for one another's benefit in the shaping of the new society which we are called upon to create.

NOTES

1. J.M. Todd, *Work*, 1960.
2. Jonathan Cape. 1979, p.2.
3. *Work in Crisis*, Edinburgh, St Andrew Press, 1983, p.209.
4. *The Coming of Post-Industrial Society*, London, Heinmann, 1974, introduction.
5. *Scientific American*, September 1982, p. 155.
6. *In Praise of Idleness*, London, Allen & Unwin, 1958, p.26.
7. In I. Clemitson and G. Rodgers, *A Life to Live*, Junction Books, 1981, p.6.
8. Penguin, 1969, p.192.
9. *Gospel in Industrial Society*, London, SCM Press, 1980, pp.44–45.
10. *Op. cit.*, pp.22–23.
11. David Bleakley, *In Place of Work*, London, SCM Press, 1968, p.44.
12. Dennis Gabor, *Inventing the Future*, Penguin, 1963, p.110.
13. A.D. Lindsay, *The Challenge of Our Time*, Contact Publications, 1948, p.71.

Work Ideologies: Prospects for Participation

PETER CRESSEY

What is a work ethic for a nation with four million unemployed? Even for the mass of people in work, the image of a self-motivated man or woman who actively seeks a career, pursues a calling or follows a vocation is a mirage.[1] Work for the majority is a highly ambiguous experience; valued for its financial and social aspects, a minimal sense of freedom from material want, an identity of sorts through a social definition of who you are. Yet the experience of work in its physical sense can be boring, achingly repetitive, exhausting and for some dangerous: within these work experiences little personal development or satisfaction is gained or expected.

In a recession, this same group of people are being told that they are lucky to have a job, whilst the reality is that such work is taken on due to the greater fear of unemployment and the dread of a meaningless, empty and dependent life-style that being jobless has come to signify.

Hence when considering the "work ethic" I start from a number of critical premises.

1. The notion of a "work ethic" that has positive elements in terms of job satisfaction and lifetime rewards is a very *restricted* one. Those members of the working population who can identify their work and individual lives as a unity of personal development are mainly professionals, academics and ministers of religion.
2. The work ethic for the rest is largely non-existent or exists in a *distorted form*, corrupted by fear, alienation or simply by the lack of an alternative. Little wonder that work becomes associated with divergent meanings; for some grinding physical work and its completion represents a masculine statement about being able to "take it" and survive. Work and masculinity are interwoven in certain occupations such as mining, trawling, construction and others. The occupational ethos redefines attitudes and breeds a form of latent sexism that surrounds and is strengthened by the current division of labour, such as to produce the male who is ashamed to be seen doing the housework or adopting a caring stance to others. Other distorted forms of the work ethic have been noted, especially

the "instrumental" attitude to work which assesses "success" only in money terms; it's not what you do but how much you earn that counts. The rationale for working which Beynon and Nichols found in their investigation of a chemicals plant was identified as an "ideology of sacrifice". The workers' time at work was sacrificed for an adequate life for the family. If the workers, usually male, made this self-sacrifice, the burden did not stop there. For the wife made her sacrifice in the home.

> She sacrifices herself for her husband and her children just as he sacrifices himself for them. It's a terrifying totality. His exploitation in the factory justifies her oppression in the home: and notions of masculinity and motherhood reinforce their mutual dependence. It is only through "sacrifice" that a wasted life has value.[2]

3. A work ethic, or the rationales that make people work or stay in meaningless and stultifying positions cannot be separated from the meanings, fears and stigmas that society attaches to being without work. There is, it seems, a dominance and primacy attached to the notion of "productive, paid work" that obscures alternative ethics emerging, ones that might shape something broader, an ethic for living for instance, where work whilst important is considered alongside involvement in community, social and other voluntary forms. The emphasis on paid work has spawned a disregard for others excluded from this sphere, hence the workless can be labelled "scrounger" whilst the housewife seemingly performs no labour at all.

If the actual process of work for the majority offers little autonomy, growth and fulfilment, the possibility has been raised that reforms or institutional paths might be created that could involve people in the aims of work, in the companies and in decision-making. Schemes for industrial democracy have been advanced as a way in which work could be given more meaning and use the latent creativity of the work-force. Post-war Europe has seen a number of schemes mooted and put into practice. British enthusiasm for industrial democracy reached its high water mark in the 1970s. The Labour government commissioned an enquiry in 1975 that reported in 1977 and become known as the Bullock report. This advocated the extension of industrial democracy through the use of worker representatives on the boards of companies. Other reforms such as developed corporate representation, the discussion of company strategy and later Labour party proposals on worker plans and planning agreements laid out the promise of greater involvement. All these mechanisms sought to promote a work-force perspective and work-force influence in the affairs and decisions that were normally closed to them. The object was to give some minimum control over the direction of the company and hence people's working lives. The change in political direction occasioned by the general election of 1979 effectively ended discussion of a general legislated reform in this area and the concept of industrial democracy, if not the problems underlying it, became *persona non grata*.

This is where my colleagues and I at Glasgow University came into the debate, undertaking research in companies during the period 1978-83. The research, of both a survey and case study kind, has looked at the extent and scope of "participation" (the term employers preferred) to see what advances have been made in developing work-forces' influence over their working lives. It is useful to divide the attempts to gain such participation into three broad camps:
1) work-force involvement in management decision-making below board level;
2) involvement in the issues surrounding the job, job satisfaction schemes, job enlargement, work humanization, etc.;
3) work-force involvement in the planning of corporate strategy, in setting the general objects of the enterprise.

The first form of participation has a wide-ranging set of proposals encased within it, ranging from works councils through consultation committees to ideas about better communications. The role of the state in promoting institutional reforms has been very important in the past, historically through the setting up of Whitley councils, the encouragement of joint consultation procedures in the civil and public sector, as well as encouraging schemes placing workers representatives on the board.

However with political change has come an emphasis on voluntary reform inside companies. The result has been an end to wider experimentation, with the public sector worker director schemes being terminated. At the same time rhetorical claims were made about increased participation through briefing groups and consultation committees. Our research in companies tends to show that little advance has been made in this area. The recession rather than bringing together employees and employers in a participative union based on common interests, has instead been fraught with problems that have actually reduced the extent and scope for consultative procedures. The recession has not led to work-forces embracing a new "realistic work ethic" but rather the bitterness and fear has resulted in open conflicts entering what were previously cooperative forms and in very many cases destroying them.

The wave of enthusiasm in the 1960s and 70s for *work humanization schemes* has largely evaporated too. The work of Trist and Emery, as well as the Tavistock Institute in Britain, did for a time suggest wide-ranging change in worker satisfaction could occur if the social and technical aspects of work organization were given sufficient thought and subsequent reform.[3] The Volvo experiments, with autonomous work-groups, and the reintroduction of group working in the mines, were signals that work could be enriched without reducing economic efficiency or returns to capital. This "socio-technical" school, as it was labelled, believed that the established division of labour was not rigidly derived from a given technological form of production, hence the alienation associated with modern work could be relieved or even abolished. With the exceptions of well-known experiments this "school" has found little real acceptance across the broad range of manufacturing and service industries. The schemes often persist in electronics, or in "islands" of production where large-scale changes have resulted in previously automated production lines becoming more group-based. The rationales behind these moves have often been primarily associated with greater profits, more flexibility and sustained production rather than with any great concern for job enrichment. In certain technical situations it makes sound economic sense to cede controls or autonomy to work-groups. Furthermore the marginality of the schemes in general terms has made their impact on a reformulated "work ethic" slight.

The group of participative proposals that seek control over work objectives are of more recent origin and tend to unite both social and industrial elements in their plans to reshape corporate objectives. Here the idea of *social need* rather than pure market forces is put forward as an organizing principle for corporate deliberations. Workers plans, alternative products and planning agreements all have this social dimension. They ask if the market, large, or multinational companies are *socially* efficient allocators and users of resources. Further, the employment and production needs of areas may be severely distorted by the current corporate strategies. The labour party is now looking for ways in which popular planning can be married with corporation decision-making in such a way that local populations and the work-forces can have an influence on the objectives and products of the various enterprises. The model for much of this style of participation has been the Lucas Aerospace workers plan for socially useful production. When faced with redundancy the work-force reacted by looking neither to confrontation or apathetic acceptance but to a scheme by which the long-term shape of the company could be altered. More recent examples that can be placed in this camp are the calls from workers in the armaments industries to draw up serious plans for converting war work into peaceful, socially needed products.[4]

These attempts at increasing participation in work do not exhaust the field; there has been continual turnover in worker cooperatives, stretching back beyond this century. There are well-known examples of self-managed companies, such as the John Lewis partnership and the Scott Bader Commonwealth. However, these areas are marginal to the experience of work for the vast number in manufacturing and service industries, and it is on these our research concentrated.

Following the withdrawal of state sponsorship of reform in the area of industrial democracy and participation, the government in the recent period has relied on "voluntarism". They have promoted a rhetoric about the need for joint approaches whilst at the same time encouraging strong leadership and resolute management. The result, unsurprisingly, is one of pessimism in industrial relations circles and the realization that effort has to be expended simply to ensure that current forms of joint consultation and discussion persist. The consultation committees and works councils that were already in existence have been under pressure as the recession has led to conflicts, suspicions and anxieties. In our case studies we have seen how this has led to the demise of such committees and the withdrawal of cooperation by work-forces. There is no evidence that recession breeds a "common approach" in which different interests are submerged in the struggle to survive. This "lifeboat democracy" theory does not hold up against the evidence of a downward spiral in trust relations within companies. What reforms one sees are limited, they are based on financial participation—profit sharing, stock dispersal aided by tax changes, or small group schemes that look to solve minor production and work problems.

In the companies not overly affected by the recession, representing various industries, novel forms are concentrated in those "sunrise industries" based on electronics; we see some continuation of work humanization via work-group activities and autonomous work-groups. The main flourish has been in relation to "quality circles" where workers volunteer to devote time to improving the quality of the product and their environment by means of projects that are accomplished through teamwork. The success of these teams was hailed as *the* way forward for worker involvement in the 80s. Once more, however, the claims and the reality have to be critically assessed. Already the first surge of enthusiasm has faltered and the failures in circles are now being reported alongside the successes.[5] The circles have tended to be sited at a low level, without access to great resources and importantly outside the normally defined "power" or authority structures within the company. Hence the impact they make is local and transitory.

The wider social form of participation through workers plans have remained largely at the level of a visionary alternative. The Lucas Aerospace example did produce a detailed and costed programme within which they identified some 150 products all of which fulfilled a social need.[6] All of them could be produced with the existing technical skills and machinery. However, its direct challenge to managerial and state control of spending and production soon ruled it unacceptable (to a Labour government of the time). More recent plans from Vickers workers to convert from tanks to consumer goods, the campaign against Polaris being built at Barrow, and the job survey of the area around Faslane and Coulport, indicate a new direction and no more. For conversion plans do need a great deal of detailed work and widespread support from the work-force. In the current uncertain climate *secure* work on weapons is being contrasted to *promises* of work on more rewarding products. In these circumstances it is the latter that is being rejected firmly by the work-forces as utopian and unrealistic. Whether this will change given an economic upswing or state backing for such conversion plans, remains to be seen.

Conclusion

If we are seeking ways in which an "alternative work ethic" can be implanted or nurtured from the embryonic forms found in industry today, then we must consider what reforms are appropriate and which have the potential to break down narrow, market defined ideas about work and its meaning for the individual enterprise and society. An honest look at the present situation leads one to a pessimistic outlook; the 80s may be a decade of stasis or even regression for work reform. The empirical situation has a number of disturbing features:

— There is greater anxiety within work-forces over job security. This has led to attitudes that give priority to measures of job protection above all others. Hence when asked about priorities, increased worker participation comes a long way down the list. The pattern that emerges in this research and in relation to changes in new technology suggests that if job guarantees are given then this acts as a kind of threshold above which cooperative relationships are possible and strengthened. However, the number able to offer such guarantees is small given the economic climate faced by British industry.

— The recession has led to a strengthening of the hierarchical form of management. The area and scope of joint discussion has narrowed whilst claims about manager rights to manage are uppermost. Notable here is an increasing centralization of decision-making: whereas previously it might have been difficult to influence company policy at a plant or divisional level, now it is virtually impossible. Decisions are fed down the line with little regard for prior consultation or for gaining the consent of the work-force to the changes being proposed.

— The picture within companies shows an increase in sectional struggles, where one group of workers in an attempt to defend their position cut across or directly come into conflict with other workgroups within the same company. So much so that in some cases work-groups are demanding cuts in other sections rather than accept them in their area. In these circumstances, a concerted and agreed

alternative plan for the enterprise will be difficult to sustain.
— The reinvigoration of market criteria is very evident, inasmuch as previously social or welfare items may have been valued in terms of benefits to both the worker and the company image. Now the attitude is "if the figures don't add up" then the change cannot be contemplated. The sort of relationship that remains is one based firmly on the "cash nexus" rather than one surrounded by paternalistic or progressive thinking.
— Treating these trends collectively, one sees a change in the treatment of work-forces and their representatives. Previously in bargaining terms and in situations of change the representatives were counselled and their advice sought. There was a recognition of the rights to representation, and equality of sorts was afforded by the involvement of representatives in the bargaining process. In general terms there is a sense that "the enemy within" has been identified as those self-same people. The kinds of partnership that were sought in the 60s and 70s are increasingly being jettisoned in favour of new authoritarian stances that echo styles developed in the nationalized industries. The market advantage that recession gives is being used to directly challenge trade union rights. Added to this is a growing reliance upon legalistic forms to settle previously domestic disputes.

The trends at the national level do find resonances in companies; many managers do not wish to inaugurate such policies knowing the bitterness this engenders. However, given an often desperate economic background the "human relations" approach to industrial relations is under severe strain. In such circumstances a new "work ethic" is urgent yet unimaginable; for most the strategy is to "keep one's head down" and wait for the pendulum to swing back rather than engage in movements for reform.

NOTES

1. In the *Protestant Ethic and the Spirit of Capitalism*, Weber himself does not define the "work ethic" in such broad terms. It is for him restricted to the emergent entrepreneurial strata whose association of economic and religious values leads to the drive to accumulate. Only the received wisdom associates the work ethic with the mass of those employed. Indeed the factory system as E.P. Thompson also notes ("Time, Work, Discipline and Industrial Capitalism", *Past and Present*, No. 38) was resisted and the new forms of time discipline were instilled only after a long struggle.
2. T. Nichols and H. Beynon. *Living with Capitalism*, p.193–4 RKP, 1977.
3. See for instance, F.E. Emery, *Characteristics of Socio-Technical Systems*, Tavistock Publications No. 527 (1959). Or Trist and Banforth. "Some Social and Psychological Consequences of the Longwall Methods of Coal Getting", *Human Relations*, Vol. 4, pp.3–38.
4. For information about these proposals see M. Cooley. *Architect or Bee*. Also much of

the work for these plans was done at the Centre for Alternative Industrial Technology, North East London Polytechnic. The Vickers plan has been produced as a book by Beynon and Wainwright, entitled *The Workers Report on Vickers*, Pluto, 1980.
5. See *A Study of Quality Circle Failures*, B. Dale and S. Hayward, UMIST, Dept. of Management Science, January 1984.
6. An example of the conversion that they envisaged was switching from electronics that were used in defence establishments and aircraft, towards building kidney machines. They also assessed the need for devices that saved workers from having to operate in dangerous environments. They championed a rail-bus and a cheap and efficient water pump that could be used in third world countries.

Towards a Normative Work Ethic

GÖRAN COLLSTE

The central theme of this chapter is the relation between ethics and technology. It deals with the question: which values govern, and which values ought to govern the choice of technology? This is one way of restating the problem of the "work ethic". To give the argument some grounding in the practical problems of technical change we shall first consider some findings concerning the consequences of the computerization of industry. Secondly, we will try to interpret what has occurred in the framework of normative ethical theory based on an understanding of human needs.

Technology and choice

It is important to emphasize that technology is a result of choice. The choice is often invisible and may be made unconsciously. Therefore, it is a necessary and important task to make the alternatives, and the presuppositions behind that choice, visible. It includes identifying those who make the choices. A checklist of questions which have to be asked in the social and ethical assessment of any particular technology must include the following:

— What are the alternatives?
— What are the consequences of different alternatives?
— How do we value these consequences?
— How do we balance individual and social group interests when they are affected by the technology in different ways? That is, how do we achieve justice?

The answers to these questions, and consequently the choice of technology, presuppose both factual information and ethical reflection.

Computerization, including the use of automated office systems and robots in manufacturing, is possibly the most far-reaching and dynamic technical change occurring in the western world today. It is therefore an urgent task to monitor and evaluate the impact of these changes on

working life and culture. A start has been made in some official investigations of computerization in Sweden, thus giving the possibility of a first, tentative answer to this impact question. The consequences of the new technology so far appear to be as follows:
1. *Increased efficiency*: This goal, of course, is the main imperative for the introduction of the new technology. It is interesting to note, however, that in spite of this many systems have not yet proved to be profitable.
2. *Reduced need for employees*: This refers to the direct impact on employment in the industries using computers. (An assessment of the global employment effects of the new technology is beyond the scope of this chapter.)
3. *Health and safety*: Some dangerous and monotonous jobs have disappeared but some new monotonous jobs have appeared—for instance, jobs which involve little more than supervision of computer terminals. There are also possible new medical problems. It is suspected that when pregnant mothers spend long hours in front of a visual display unit (VDU) there are detrimental effects on the foetus.
4. *Quality of work-place relations*: Many computer systems are designed for individual work instead of group work. They therefore have the tendency to increase isolation in the work-place. However, the new technology also has potential for promoting social contacts since workers' attachment to their work-stations or machines decreases.
5. *Knowledge and skills*: There is an increased demand for knowledge and qualification levels for some workers, but a decreased demand for knowledge and an inferior level of work for others. In short, silent knowledge often disappears when work is computerized. It is the kind of everyday knowledge which cannot easily be programmed. Workers no longer know how to react in unexpected situations, and their competence to use materials and new methods based on experience disappears.
6. *Management and control*: There are increased possibilities for management to monitor and control the work process and consequently diminished possibilities for workers to participate in and direct their own work.

Even this summary list shows that the costs and benefits in economic and social terms are not susceptible to simple calculation. Further monitoring and information is necessary, but not sufficient. To attempt an evaluation requires a framework which gives a particular value or weight to the various aspects of computing and automation.

A normative ethic

For the sake of consistency, the criteria and goals which govern the choice and application of new computer-based technology will need to be related to each other in a normative ethical theory. However, in the field of ethics there are many kinds of normative theory, that is to say, theories about criteria for right action. There are deontological theories which state that actions (social institutions, social change, etc.) should not be evaluated solely by their consequences. Deontological theories posit other criteria which should be taken into account but differ in respect to what these criteria should be. According to the much discussed theory of Robert Nozick,[1] actions must be consistent with certain rights, especially property rights. John Rawls, on the other hand, in his influential book, *A Theory of Justice*,[2] develops principles of justice which ought to govern ethical choices. There are also theological versions of deontological theory. One example, sometimes called the Divine Command Theory,[3] holds that the standard of right and wrong is the will or law of God. The theological ethics of Karl Barth belongs to this category.

Another set of theories is the teleological. According to these theories it is the consequences of different ethical alternatives which are decisive. Utilitarianism, which holds that actions maximizing utility are correct, is the most common of these theories. There are, however, alternative versions of utilitarianism which have arisen among other things because of disagreement about the concept of utility. According to one version, often called preference-utilitarianism, utility is understood in terms of the actual preferences of an individual as determined by his or her behaviour.[4] However, the concept of preference in this context is, in my view, too superficial. That which is ultimately value-able must be something more basic than subjective preferences which can be manipulated in many different ways. It must in some way be related to a conception of human nature. The actual preferences of an individual can thus be in conflict with his real interest. As an alternative I suggest that actions should be assessed according to whether they promote or prevent the fulfilment of human needs. My choice of normative theory is thus a need-orientated version of utilitarianism.

Different ultimate motivations can be given for this choice. One possible base is the biblical command to love. The command to love one's neighbour can be interpreted to mean that one is also to serve his needs. Thus the love commandment can be seen as one formulation of an ethical insight that is common to all irrespective of faith or religion.

The basic concept according to this theory is *need*. A human need is that which:

a) will cause human suffering if denied;
b) is generally prevalent in all men and women;
c) is relatively constant over time.

Need-gratification is thus fundamental to our wellbeing.

The Finnish philosopher Georg H. von Wright has pointed out the intersubjective character of the concept of need. He makes a comparison with the "needs" of plants. A plant needs, among other things, light, air and water. If these needs are not gratified up to a certain minimum level, the plant dies. If they are not gratified up to a higher level, it will languish; however, if the plant receives what it needs, it will prosper. "Languish" and "prosper" in this context are not value-concepts. One can in an empirical way determine if a plant is languishing or prospering. And the connection between the necessary condition for a plant to prosper and its prosperous state, is a causal connection that can be confirmed by botanists.

According to von Wright one can in a similar way assume that human beings have certain needs that have to be gratified in order for them to survive and "prosper". To survive, men and women need certain amounts of air and nutrition and certain social relationships to prosper. For them to be able to live a good life, a large proportion of their physiological, social and psychological needs have to be gratified.[5] Whether it is *desirable* that human beings should be able to gratify their needs is, of course, a normative question. However, the value judgement one has to make—that it is desirable that they should survive and prosper—is not controversial. This normative theory implies a demand for equality. Since human needs are common to all human beings, each person has the same right of access to the means of gratification.

The empirical task of defining the needs which have to be met if human beings are to survive and prosper is one for the human sciences including psychology and sociology. Using the results of research in these disciplines,[6] I propose the following list of human needs:

a) physiological or primary needs (food, water, air etc.);
b) psychological or social needs:
   — safety;
   — community (love, affection, social contacts);
   — self-respect (grounded both in self-confidence and in other people's esteem of oneself);
   — comprehension and consistency (acquiring an understanding of reality, a coherent world-view);
   — self-realization (using and developing one's innate resources and gifts);
   — autonomy (controlling one's life, self-determination).

There is a difference between the physiological needs on the one hand and the psychological and social needs on the other in terms of the conditions for their gratification. The gratification of the physiological needs depends to a great extent on external conditions including climatic conditions, possibilities for cultivation, political and economic systems etc. Gratification of psychological and social needs depends more on individuals themselves. Various circumstances may facilitate or inhibit social contact, but at best they can only provide the setting in which the giving and receiving of love can take place and grow.

To say that each individual has a *right* to have his or her needs for self-respect and community gratified may seem strange when the gratification of these needs depends to a certain extent on individuals themselves. What is being suggested here is that one has a right to have those needs which can be gratified by external means fulfilled and a right to those external conditions which are necessary for the gratification of the other needs, which can be met by human action.

The different needs vary in importance. The physiological needs are of a more urgent nature but become subordinate when a certain degree of gratification has been reached. This fact, therefore, makes it possible to specify certain priority rules in the proposed normative theory:

1. In cases where the gratification of the physiological needs of one or more persons is found to remain under a certain level, "the x-level", an alternative best fitted to increase the physiological wellbeing of those concerned ought to be chosen.
2. When all the individuals have reached the x-level, priority ought to be given to measures providing the necessary means of meeting the psychological and social needs of the individuals.

These priority rules, however, do not give an adequate answer to the question of how to give a weighting to the level of need-gratification of the different individuals affected by an action. Let me illustrate this with an example: assume that one is required to choose between alternative actions, A and B, where as a consequence of A, n persons will end up below and y persons will end up above the x-level, and as a consequence of B, n + y persons end up below, but the total sum of need-gratification will be greater in B than in A, since n + y is nearer the x-level in B than n in A. To be able to make a choice between A and B, one has to rely on further priority rules. If one follows the theory of justice elaborated by Rawls one will choose the alternative that benefits the least advantaged members of society, which is alternative A. If, on the other hand, one follows utilitarianism, one will choose the alternative that maximizes the total sum of need-gratification, which is alternative B.

Theory and practice

It is, of course, not a simple task to apply this kind of normative theory to political, economic and technical changes and alternatives. I will restrict myself to an outline sketch of an evaluation of the new technology. Despite its brevity it will show that a normative ethical theory can be applied to practical decision-making.

1. Increased efficiency will probably enhance possibilities for the gratification of material *demands* but not needs, while the basic physiological needs are already gratified in a high-consumption society like Sweden.
2. The new technology seems to have both positive and negative effects on the possibilities for workers to achieve self-respect and self-realization. For some, the quality of work is increasing, while for others it is decreasing. Computerization, therefore, seems to lead to polarization. So far, however, the effects seem to have been primarily negative for the majority of workers, because they have led to decreased skills for work.
3. The new technology also seems in spite of its potential to have undermined the occupational and work-place community by increasing the isolation of workers from each other.
4. Even the potential for greater autonomy that computer systems can provide seems to be cancelled out because of the increasing possibilities for management to direct and control the work process.

At the risk of oversimplifying, the effects could be summarized in the following sentence: The possibilities for gratifying material demands have increased as a result of the new technology, while the possibilities for gratifying psychological and social needs have decreased. How far this is true is, of course, an empirical question. However, it can be informed by ethical criteria which can be used in developing alternatives as well as in evaluation of present trends. These effects of computerization are not unavoidable. The power of computers to process data and information is like electricity: it can be used in many different ways and for many different purposes. So far the market has been paramount in the introduction of the new technology. If new technology is to promote the fulfilment of human needs to a greater extent than hitherto, future developments have to be controlled accordingly in the light of this goal.

The question then arises: who should be responsible for controlling the direction of new technology? From a Swedish viewpoint, with its corporatist structures and powerful labour organization, it is natural to answer "the trade unions". However, it is a hard task to control the introduction of new technology when computer systems, for the most part, are imported and give little room for modification and alternative designs. This fact has stimulated efforts to design new computer systems in cooperation with the workers who will use them. The starting point is to determine what the workers themselves require and then design systems on the basis of these requirements.[7] This is a path which will have to be followed—and should be followed—if in contrast to so much past technology, it is to promote the wellbeing of those who use it. A new "work ethic", therefore, is not just about changing values and attitudes which are no longer appropriate to an age of computing and highly automated systems—it is a practical step towards achieving a more humane technology and a more responsible society because of a more involved work-force.

NOTES

1. *Anarchy, State and Utopia*, Oxford, 1974.
2. London, 1976.
3. W. Frankena, *Ethics*, New York, 1973, p.28.
4. T.J. Beauchamp & N.E. Bowie, *Ethical Theory and Business*, Englewood Cliffs, 1979, p.6.
5. "Om behov.", *Filosofisk Tidskrift*, No. 1, 1982.
6. See e.g. E. Fromm, *Man for Himself*, New York, 1947; *The Sane Society*, New York, 1955. A. Maslow, *Motivation and Personality*, New York, 1954. A. Etzioni, *The Active Society*, New York, 1968.
7. See *The Utopia-Project: on Training, Technology and Products Viewed from the Quality of Work Perspective*, Arbetslivscentrum (Swedish Center for Working Life), 1981.

PART IV
Conclusions

Tasks for the Churches

1. Industrial Communities in Decline

The majority of contributions have had a medium- or long-term perspective which tries to envisage the possibilities for future society and the steps in the transition. In contrast, the focus of this report is the present; the issue of "how people live their lives now". It starts from the present crisis, a tragedy which is unfolding daily in Glasgow and many other cities throughout western Europe where much traditional mass-employment industry is on the decline, or has already disappeared. Whatever the future trends in technology, education and policy a response is called for *now*. Not only do great numbers of people suffer in the present, but our ability to start planning for the future we want depends on our being able to intervene constructively to remove the obstacles which stand in the way.

The immediate crisis has many features which are recognizable across national boundaries. The experience of Glasgow, Duisburg, Milan and countless other manufacturing industrial areas is community-wide unemployment. The circumstances which create unemployment are linked to environmental deterioration and decline in public services which few in the community can escape from. In these situations it is scarcely an exaggeration to talk of a "culture of unemployment".

The general sense of impotence in the face of industrial decline is made all the greater by the knowledge that for a very substantial number of people there are no jobs, and there will be no jobs in the foreseeable future. In some communities, this fundamental lack of choice drives many of those with specialized, marketable skills elsewhere, leaving the unskilled behind. One of the effects is to destroy the accumulated experience of the community. Apart from the human and social costs, the economic costs of high unemployment are all too obvious, yet it is surprising how even the direct cost of an unemployed person (about £6,600 p.a. in the UK) is ignored in calculations of economic performance on a national scale. In areas of industrial decline, there is a striking paradox in the fact that despite the loss of traditional employment (and the claim that no other work is available) the people concerned are in a situation of crying need for work to be done—in housing, environmental development, social care, education, etc.

Finally, for much of the rest of the population—and sadly, the church—the crisis in these areas of industrial decline is like something happening on another planet. It is not a part of everyday experience and responsibility. However, since these are the people with the resources, the votes and the will to change policy, their responsibility is inescapable.

This view of the present "community" crisis in the traditional mass employment areas, contrasts strongly with the assumption which appears to underly the prevailing employment policies: in particular the assumption that the national interest is to be equated with maximum efficiency and competitiveness, and that unemployment is therefore inevitable but only temporary, the costs being borne by individuals according to their position in the labour market. A personal setback, but a stimulus to greater effort.

It is clear that these assumptions are unacceptable in a community-centred analysis of the situation. For instance, to say without qualification that economic efficiency is in the national interest fails to look beyond a very narrow set of financial criteria to the actual human costs and needs of the situation and the wider understanding of a "good" and not merely competitive society. To assume that unemployment is temporary contrasts sharply with the empirical observation of large numbers permanently without work, for whom there will be no work in the foreseeable future. This reality speaks of the desperate plight of people, not facts and figures; about the quality of life, not the quality of graphs. Our response is primarily a call to the church and to society to see this situation as its agenda for the present, not merely substance for theoretical discussion about the future.

Confronted and challenged by the needs of people and communities in areas of industrial decline, the churches have to begin by recognizing their own failure to give anything approaching an adequate Christian response, and this over a period of two hundred years at least. Not only have the churches in these areas done little more than apply first aid in certain circumstances; not only have they betrayed the gospel with their too ready proclamation of an other-worldly pietism; not only have they acted for far too long as if they could deal with the situation by themselves, and had some divine mandate to do so; but increasingly over the last fifty years they have tended to withdraw from such areas, pulling their resources of leadership, plant and human capacity back to areas where they hope to receive a "better" return for their investment. There are exceptions to this, and we recognize and salute them. By and large they are too little, and very late.

We see at least three responses which we believe the churches should make in areas of decline—and in some cases these are already being made.

a) For too long the churches in these areas have been attempting to opt "for" the poor; thus, they have developed structures and styles of worship, organization and leadership which are in the main paternalistic, involve little participation, and which are imposed from behind or from without, with little or no attention given to the needs of the people and the circumstances of their lives. And they have felt it satisfactory to continue to do this in their separate denominations.

We believe a more adequate response would be for the churches in such areas to unite in local efforts, and to listen to the poor. To know people is to listen—to hear them as they are—to take their concerns seriously. This would encourage the existing growth, or promote new growth, of informal churches in parallel with the formal institutional structures, and ensure that such churches are not "for" as much as "of" the poor, with characteristics of local leadership, small-scale, and cross-denominational membership.

b) At the same time we have noted that in many denominations the concern at the local level has primarily been for the shepherding of the sheep within the fold, in direct contradiction to the evangelical command to care more for those outside. Such caring, however, when it has taken place, has tended not to recognize people's real needs or the fold's real problems.

We believe the churches have a continuing responsibility, particularly in areas of industrial decline, to work alongside women and men of goodwill, in order that the structures of community, so severely threatened in the present climate, may be strengthened and adapted to meet the ever-changing situation. We believe these structures include not simply the formal community structures (political groups, housing associations, tenants associations, etc.) but also the informal ones (workers cooperatives, credit unions, unemployed workers centres, etc.).

c) One of the most difficult things for people in such areas to understand is what is actually going on, and which forces can be trusted and which should be resisted in the turmoil of change.

A valid criticism of the churches in relation to such areas is that they have failed fully to try to understand what is happening, or, where they have tried and succeeded, they have failed to communicate that understanding effectively to the people in these threatened communities.

We believe that the churches must intensify their struggle to understand the forces at work in our society: that they must be constantly on guard against the danger of collusion with demonic forces: that they must always seek to challenge or commend on the basis of detailed information, with honesty towards their own structures as well; and that they must increasingly seek to find more effective ways of sharing their findings at a local and congregational level.

Recommendations
1. The primary theological theme in response to the present situation of industrial decline should be justice and the restoration of right relationships within society. The churches must not preach this without being committed to redistributing their own resources and reordering their structures in favour of the poor.
2. The churches will only become more committed through listening to the poor and becoming better informed about the plight of people and communities in areas of industrial decline. They must join with those who are resisting the forces of destruction in their communities.
3. Churches must work together to encourage and develop new patterns of informal church groupings in areas of industrial decline.
4. Theologians should re-emphasize the corporate responsibility of men and women for one another arising out of the command to love. This should include detailed study of the Old Testament understanding of the corporate salvation of Israel and other relevant themes.

2. The Social Impact of New Technologies

Enthusiasm and fearful resistance represent polar attitudes to the "micro-electronic era". Distinctively Christian voices in this arena have been muted or absent. What follows is an attempt to bring together some description of the significant areas affected by the "impact of micro-electronics", an analysis of some of the assumptions underlying the rapid commercial diffusion of these new applications, some pointers to a Christian critique of current attitudes and practice in this field, and some practical proposals, particularly in relation to policy and education.

Smaller and cheaper electronic equipment, made possible by the silicon chip, has led to a scramble for new and lucrative markets. It also makes possible the convergence of computing with telecommunications, known together as "information technology". Industry and commerce may gain much in efficiency and productivity through such new applications, and there are also obvious benefits in medicine and education. However, the military emphasis in research and development involves a bias against such useful applications. Domestic benefits are less obvious; much micro-electronic trivia floods the market.

The impact of all this is felt in various ways. We believe that it is myopic to focus only on the employment effects, especially at the societal level, difficult as they are to interpret. Mass unemployment is due now to world recession, not micro-electronics, but the latter is no empty threat. Robotization and office automation do displace labour. Hi-tech industries will not be big employers in the future. Drudgery may indeed be eliminated, but the scale of job dislocation demands adjustment policies to cope with it. The other effects are felt in the following spheres:

a) *Politics*: State surveillance has risen steadily over the past two hundred years, but the networking of data-bases of personal information makes the *Nineteen-Eighty-Four* warnings very relevant. This development precedes so-called computer democracy, which could be realized through interactive cabling systems.

b) *Culture*: Various items fall into this category, including addictive and vindictive computer games, and also the boost given by the spread of computers to "algorithmic thinking", the tendency to imagine that all kinds of problems—even moral or philosophical ones—are in principle solvable by the appropriate technique.

c) *Society*: This impact is far more difficult to judge, Alvin Toffler's "electronic cottage" notwithstanding. Like many other technologies micro-electronics has great potential for human liberation and human enslavement.

d) *Economy*: "Information" is increasingly being treated like a commodity, controlled by those with access to it. An "information-rich/information-poor" division is emerging in parallel with the divisions within the labour market.

e) *Management and control of work*: "Deskilling" is an important effect of micro-electronic development, seen in computer-aided design, computer numerical control, word processing, and so on. Questions are raised about the relationship between human judgment and practical experience on the one hand, and the unconscious activity of the machine on the other. Some doubt that there are limits to this displacement of human knowledge and labour.

Control of the labour-force is another self-confessed motive of managers installing micro-electronic equipment. It is an extension of Taylorism which inhibits the development of skills, autonomy, cooperation, personal responsibility and initiative.

f) *Global relations*: Both the astonishing new possibilities opened up by techniques like direct broadcasting by satellite, and the fact that the biggest hi-tech companies are transnationals, contributing to the new international division of labour, bring home the rapid globalization process of the late twentieth century.

A number of popular beliefs, expressed implicitly or explicitly in the media, advertising, or in government reports, are based on technical, economic and social assumptions which are open to question. The beliefs about technology include:
— the assumed inevitability of technical change, the view that innovation will continue into the foreseeable future, bringing rapid, continuous and far-reaching change;

— the belief that "technical fixes" will be found to solve any unforeseen problems which arise from technological development;
— the idea that change is progress, that technological advance is always desirable, in that the human condition is improved thereby;
— the supposition that technology is neutral, that the effects for good or bad are dependent only on the "application"; the social shaping of the technology itself is ignored.

Current economic thinking includes the assumption that economic decline is the result of a failure to be competitive, and that adaptation to the micro-electronic age is the only answer. The slogan "automate or liquidate" sums this up perfectly. Also, it is taken to be axiomatic that growth for profit is the over-riding aim in the adoption of new technology.

Finally social assumptions are made concerning worker flexibility. The adaptability of workers in relation to skills, mobility and training is expected by industry and government. Unwillingness is interpreted as irrational. In all of this official "ideology" which could be said to be forming the basis of a new "work ethic", technological utopia is just around the corner, after a brief period of disturbance. This is the "post-industrial" or "information society", which will result from unregulated technological development for profit. Thus, although there are really no choices before us (no one actually wants technological regression or liquidation), we are advised not to worry. A bright, hi-tech/hi-touch future awaits us.

One of the priorities in Christian reflection on work and the future should be a critique of these increasingly powerful beliefs. The recurring themes are creation and idolatry. Christian reflection on technology draws us back to our origins. We affirm that God is Creator, and that we creatures, made in God's image, are corporately accountable to God alone. In the task of serving, stewarding and participating in creation we use tools—technology—in line with the directive to love and serve God and neighbour. However, history and experience confirm the biblical account of the breakdown of the Creator/creature balance which begins with human declarations of independence. Ceasing to expect God to act, people become self-centred, and also turn to idols. One of today's manifestations of this is the idolizing of new technology. Forgetting God, something within the creation is treated as if it were Creator, and assumed to have a life of its own. Means become ends, and trust and hope are invested in them. Answers are sought from technology. The churches may collude in this idolatry.

In Christ lies hope of liberation from idolatry, and for recall to origins. Neighbour-love should be seen in Christian community, which is based on communion with Christ and affects all our communication.

The fragmentation, dehumanization and manipulation of people by technology should be actively resisted in the name of Christ. Personal, local, and global wholeness (*shalom*) should be our aim. Creatures are accountable to the Creator, and this relates directly to our technological praxis as we anticipate the new creation.

Recommendations

Different levels of response are called for, depending on whether one is relating to technology's promoters, decision-makers, or "recipients". The churches can help by listening, supporting, and challenging.

1. A priority for Christian reflection and study is a critique of dominant assumptions, such as those mentioned above, and a challenge to the misleading idea that hi-tech development will mean a return to full employment.
2. A priority for Christian action is to promote new social policies which are integrated with technological and economic strategies. The realization that there are losers in today's zero-sum games should lead to humanized policy decisions. This also includes special social assistance to regions which have "declining industries", and the allowance of sufficient transition periods when new technology is introduced.
3. The churches should work with other bodies to encourage independent "social monitoring" to assess new technologies not only as commodities, but also for their ethical tolerability.
4. An urgent educational task is to inform the churches and the general public about the real choices confronting us, and the potential effects of new technology on individual human lives and societies. There is an urgent need for a critical bibliography which would help to counter hi-tech/information society propaganda.
5. The churches must encourage continued dialogue between theologians and industrialists and cooperation between church and industry in industrial chaplaincies to assist individuals in high technology occupations as they struggle to follow the leading of the spirit.

3. Youth, Education and Training

Rapid technical and social change gives great urgency to questions about the practice of education and the values which guide it. These include:
— Who are, and who should be, the beneficiaries of the education system?

— What are education and training for?
— What are the relative merits of "work-centred" models compared with "life-centred" models?

Given the shifts in economic activity and employment resulting from the introduction of new technology and the decline of heavy industries, the "work-centred" education/training model seems increasingly inappropriate. While work-based education and training can be very effective in motivating youngsters who can move on into jobs and careers in which their newly-acquired skills and training are directly applied, it cannot meet the needs of all young people. Any policy restricted to this approach fails the substantial numbers of young people who cannot realistically expect to find suitable employment in the short or medium term.

Group reflection on personal educational histories proved to be most helpful in identifying crucial issues. We identified a number of qualities—some learned at school, others not—which we agreed should be the accepted norm within a "life-centred" education for all children in a compassionate society. It was felt that these qualities could be fostered through a creative approach to learning which recognizes the value of these individual attributes to personal development and learning. These qualities, not arranged in any order of importance, are: initiative; independence; responsibility for self and others; satisfaction; competence; self-respect; respect for others' needs; decision-taking; awareness; dignity; constructive application of competitive spirit; compassion; physical/mental health; inventiveness and creative qualities; ability to collaborate and cooperate; respect for individual freedom.

By "life-centred" education we mean a system of learning through which skills and knowledge are imparted to equip future citizens for productive and meaningful existence, with or without paid employment, and with the means to participate fully in the decision-making processes. Within such a system the above qualities would provide the essential framework around which skills and knowledge could be successfully built. We have no wish to deny the importance of knowledge for its own sake, but recognize the need for the individuals to see knowledge as directly relevant to their personal existence, as a force for personal and social liberation.

The response in many European countries to youth unemployment has been to create special training and work experience programmes. These tend to have a narrower purpose than the above values imply. Youth training schemes (YTS) in the UK, for instance, have attracted the following serious criticisms:

1. They use young people as cheap and substitute labour, suppressing youth wage rates.
2. The quality and monitoring of schemes is often questionable.

Tasks for the Churches

3. Health and safety standards are not always respected.
4. Many YTS trainees do not gain experience of constructive trade union activity. They are powerless and vulnerable, with no means of becoming organized or of making themselves heard.
5. YTS is essentially short-term work experience and is not a policy for combatting long-term youth unemployment.
6. The majority of YTS schemes are employment orientated. Should this continue to the case given the fact that many youngsters will not experience employment?
7. The opportunities for work experience obtained by youngsters on YTS are determined by local provision in industry and commerce. In areas of industrial decline provision is impoverished and hence the quality of training is affected. Moreover youngsters in such areas seldom proceed to full-time work with the employer who provided the work experience, as do trainees in locations with higher levels of employment.

In the light of our understanding of the theology and ethics of work we considered our own experiences and perceptions. Work which appears to have no purpose denies individual dignity yet even the most menial and unpleasant tasks can be carried out without loss of dignity, if such tasks are not restricted through discrimination to the more vulnerable members of the community. However, the hierarchies and division of labour in our society create few opportunities for such demonstrations of social responsibility. Certain groups bear the burden of menial and unpleasant tasks.

The size of an organization affects the extent to which the individual can play a significant part. Whilst the number of small businesses is increasing, this is still an important consideration for the training of young people—many of whom will be employed by large organizations and bureaucracies in the public sector. We are not aware of any training initiatives to prepare youngsters especially for making an effective contribution within such structures. In fact, there might be incentives for bureaucracies to encourage workers' participation in times of economic stringency. If an organization is too large for individual work roles to be seen as meaningful, we see a loss of self-respect. An individual obtains a sense of self worth when the personal contribution to the whole can be perceived, and when there are opportunities for personal creativity, if only in the peripheral context, for example in improving working conditions and work-based leisure activities.

Much of the contemporary reality of employment and unemployment is very far removed from the traditional Christian view of "vocation". There is a need for open debate within the churches on these issues. The unemployed, housewives, and younger people within the church community should be asked to share their experiences. In many church communities unemployment does not yet pose a direct problem. Such communities need to search for means of raising awareness and encouraging a practical response. The reality of the crisis facing unemployed people could be effectively communicated by inviting unemployed people from areas which are badly hit to discuss such experiences with their contemporaries elsewhere. Attitudes towards women who stay at home to care for their children and families are revealing. This is not paid work, and so is not accorded the status which would be given to workers in paid employment carrying a similar responsibility.

More importantly, our present system of values undervalues the work of women and of others in the caring professions. Qualities such as openness, cooperation, and compassion are not compatible with the "masculine" work ethic which currently prevails. The present system of values gives credence and reward to competition, aggression, and oppression, and discourages the expression of less assertive characteristics. This is emotionally damaging to men and women alike, creating a prison in which all are to some extent confined. The key to our emotional freedom lies in a shift of values such that men and women recognize the fundamental importance of the ability to care for and share with others.

"Work" could then become that contribution made by an individual for the maintenance, support or enrichment of the life of the community. Wealth-creating employment on the international, national and local basis would obviously still be crucial, and qualities of competition and assertiveness would continue to play a part. But all would recognize the limitations in terms of manpower requirements for this aspect of our economy, and the equal value of the contributions of the majority not within this sector. Education and training will necessarily play a crucial part in achieving these goals.

Anne's story

("Anne's Story", the narrative description of an unemployed person's experience, is a dramatic symbol of the need and the opportunity which is facing the churches. Anne Monaghan, who participated in the workshop, is a young unemployed teacher living in Glasgow.)

"When I saw the poster advertising a film show in the church hall the following night, I was vaguely interested. I mean it made a change for them to do something other than Mothers' Union Meetings and wee ladies socials. It was about the Philippines. Anyway, it was free and it would make a change from sitting about at Lynne's or going for another walk to the chippy. That's always dead depressing. That's where all the junkies hang about and some of them were junior to me at school. It was getting really boring these days, having nothing to do. Even when I do have cash there's not a lot to do anyway; just the same places and the same faces. Nothing exciting ever seems to happen these days. Everything's just the same—dead boring. Even the youth training scheme (YTS) was hopeless.

"First of all, I worked in this architect's office where I was really talked down to by this man in charge. He was always criticizing something about me—if it wasn't my clothes, it was my hair, or my time-keeping or my attitude. I got really sick of that—who did he think he was? All they ever let me do was work at the switchboard and I didn't know how to work it because nobody showed me, until Cathy did. She was really nice, the only person in that dump that treated me like a human. She used to stick up for me. She even gave me a present when I was moving on to the hairdressers.

"That was another joke. Twenty-five quid (£25) a week to sweep up hair all day long, except, of course, when we were allowed to wash the customers' hair; they made that seem like a privilege. The clients were quite interesting, though, and sometimes you could have a really good chat. Still, that didn't make up for the boredom. There was a crowd of YTSs working there but for some reason they were really unfriendly towards me, not that I had anything in common with them. They were always whispering about the customers, the manageress, the job, the pay, but they would never say anything out loud about the things they said they hated.

"One day, the manageress got us all into her office to tell us all off for being so unfriendly and so unhelpful and she singled me out and started saying she'd never seen me smile. Everybody was looking at me and I felt really embarrassed and blurted out: Well, what do you expect? After that she really had it in for me. I had been dead keen to do hairdressing but in two months the most I'd done was mix up dyes once or twice.

"I started to miss work and meet my pal instead. She was a YTS too, and hated it more than I did. Anyway, we both knew we would never get kept on because the bosses didn't like us. Obviously, I didn't tell my parents I wasn't going to work because it would have been unbearable. My mum and dad were always nagging on at me as it was, and telling me they couldn't understand me—that I was so selfish and inconsiderate. They had even started saying I was odd, that it seemed I didn't want to work. What they couldn't understand was that I was slaving every day for the same money I'd get for doing nothing, like some of my friends. In fact, I was paying more than I could afford for bus fares! I still pay half fare on the buses these days but it's getting harder to get away with. The way I look at it is, I haven't got enough money to waste on bus fares so I might as well. I don't see it as cheating or stealing or anything.

"Anyway, it didn't take long to get caught skipping work. One night when I got home, my boss telephoned, and there was a big battle in the house. In fact, they threatened to throw me out so I just walked out and stayed with my friend that night. It seemed to do some good because they seemed more relieved than angry when I went back home. I'd had enough. I walked out of the YTS and I couldn't get any unemployment money for six weeks because I had left the scheme. The fights started in the house again but because I had so much time, I would tidy up and do dishes and clean—just for something to do—and I noticed that my mum started talking to me differently. I think she felt sorry for me. Sometimes I still get upset when people start acting sympathetic—I mean, I don't need their pity.

"Anyway, my pal and I went to this film which was really good. It was about the awful conditions which people in the Philippines lived under—working really long hours and hardly being paid. Their living conditions were worse than ours. A priest got some land and gave it to these people to work on as their own. They learned how to grow crops and things and they shared work, food and chores and they all had something to live for. It turned out that the priest who'd bought the land for the peasants had been framed along with eight others on murder charges and they went to prison.

"After the film there was a discussion. I was surprised to hear some of the older people's reactions, saying things about this area and the unfairness and the poverty that I didn't realize they'd ever noticed, although, thinking about it, they'd been around a lot longer than me, and I realized they must have experienced things I'm experiencing.

"It also turned out that the film show had been organized by a new Christian action group. I nearly died when I saw some of the people in this group: the woman upstairs from my granny and the guy who works in the social security office, my pal's uncle—they all seem dead different from each other—but to hear them talk, they all had something in common—concern. I couldn't help feeling dead emotional when I thought about it. Maybe we all have one thing in common, something to share. Maybe it's just finding common ground that's holding us back.

"I wondered if maybe we could do some things around this area. The Philippines is all very well, but there's plenty to be done here too, maybe—like helping the junkies at the chip shop by getting them interested in something and organizing other events and groups that would appeal to people like me. I'm still bored, but I felt different that night among all the people. It would be good to have more things where the local people can get involved. I even have second thoughts about what the church is all about."

Recommendations
1. The churches must examine their own attitudes and policy towards youth, education and training to ensure that children are brought

up to exercise self-responsibility for their skills and talents within and outside paid employment.
2. Churches in areas of low unemployment must educate themselves in the problems and opportunities of changing employment structures and take practical steps to show that they value persons in themselves, not according to their standing in paid employment.
3. Churches in areas of high unemployment must cooperate to provide mutual support and encouragement in their outreach to the unemployed. Local initiatives (unemployed workers' centres, self-help groups, youth work, etc.) should involve close links with non-church agencies where appropriate.

The following resolutions were also passed by the workshop plenary:
a) This workshop requests Church and Society, the Ecumenical Development Cooperative Society, the Society, Religion and Technology Project and other relevant church bodies such as the Iona Community in Scotland to investigate the feasibility of establishing a cooperative industrial enterprise in Scotland along the lines of the Derry Project recently supported by EDCS. We affirm that it is in such action as this that the prophetic witness of the church should take form today.
b) This workshop recommends to the WCC that in the future programme of Church and Society, common cause be made with the sub-unit on Women in Church and Society, in the examination of social values, work ethics and theology.

4. International Strategies

The following report does not seek to be comprehensive but rather to point to some of the problems, opportunities and strategies involved in the international response to high technology.

High technology is not a neutral process; its development has to be seen in the context of economic and political trends which characterize the relation between and within nations. High technology has, or will have, a considerable impact on politics, economy and society. High technology considered as an instrument inducing drastic changes in our societies must be evaluated according to the following criteria:
— Does it answer to the real needs of humankind?
— Does it foster a better sharing of resources?
— Does it promote through information and communication real participation?
— Does it contribute to the integrity of creation?

We turn now to consider the problems and opportunities presented by the rapid growth in high technology, and possible working strategies.

Problems

Research and development for high technology industries is concentrated in very few countries. This leads to the promotion of interests which are both too narrow and too short-term.

The wider social implications of the establishment of high technology industries are often not considered. The social needs of local populations can be quite unrelated to these developments.

There is a clear need for the sharing of information between groups of people who work in the same industry, or even the same transnational company, but who tend to have relevant information withheld from them. The churches should be instrumental in working towards the establishment of better channels of communication.

The overwhelming concentration of resources geared to the development of weapons and armaments remains a matter of great concern. It is well known that a small fraction of the same resources could meet the most urgent needs of the less developed countries.

Though governments in both the so-called developed and developing countries may justify their cooperation in the establishment of high technology industries as being in the local interest, it is often necessary to question these assumptions. In particular questions should be asked about the long-term transferability of these technologies in these locations.

Opportunities

When developed properly, high technology industries have the capacity to remove drudgery, improve health and lengthen life expectancy. They can widen horizons and enable ordinary people to gain access to vital information. The uses and spread of new technologies can heighten awareness and reduce isolation among the world's peoples, e.g. by low-powered village radios, etc.

Technology makes available a number of beneficial tools which can be used to overcome otherwise inexorable problems. For example, these might include better environmental monitoring and erosion control.

In some already developed countries we recognize the availability of the products of the new technology as having potential for reducing some of the worst effects of industrial decline and unemployment. We welcome the prospect of more flexible patterns of working.

We encourage the WCC to build up a data base of relevant activities and information (e.g. community-based employment initiatives) which would be made available to churches, agencies and the media on a worldwide basis and at a low cost. This recognizes the WCC as a source of vital information which could be more widely used through new technological means.

We encourage the WCC's member churches to become involved in programmes of education to help their members recognize both the problems and the opportunities being created by the introduction of high technology.

Strategies

There is a growing and powerful international movement for peace and economic justice which is bringing together through trade unions, churches and voluntary peace pressure groups people concerned about mass unemployment, a growing concentration of wealth in the hands of the powerful few, and the disastrous waste of resources being ploughed into armaments research and weapons production.

This movement has brought to light what is being done in national settings towards "conversion" work—that is, changing the end products of factories to socially acceptable and life-enhancing products instead of weapons. As a result of a recent conference where ideas for conversion were exchanged, a trade union in the US believes it can save four hundred jobs threatened because of a slow-down in the nuclear reactor turbine industry.

When this "alternative" thinking is applied to developing countries more concrete ideas come to the fore. The World Health Organization estimates that five million children die each year from six diseases—measles, dyphtheria, tetanus, whooping cough, polio and tuberculosis. Cheap mass production methods for vaccine and immunization have been developed and it is now possible to immunize all these children against them. Workers in instrument industries could produce simple refrigeration plants for storing vaccines.

There is a need for strong, repairable buses—a job for former car workers. There is a need for basic universal agricultural equipment. Pumps are constantly required for irrigation schemes. Another idea put forward at a meeting of the International Metal Workers Federation is for those in shipbuilding and heavy construction to be building large scale solar activated desalination plants. Tools For Self-Reliance re-cycles unwanted tools from the UK to other parts of the world. The list is almost endless.

This type of operation must be developed in a way which is mutually supportive and just. The will to do this is growing within the groups mentioned. The political will, however, is still lacking. Governments should be encouraged to explore at world levels through the UN, the ILO and on a bilateral basis how these creative ideas from the work-force can be made into viable employment-creating projects.

Recommendations
1. The churches must seek ways of improving channels of communication between groups of people who work in the same industry or company in more than one country, especially when these workers have relevant information withheld from them.
2. As a major centre of worldwide communication between churches, the WCC should consider establishing a data base of relevant activities and information for access by churches, agencies and the media.
3. The churches must develop programmes of education to assist their members in recognizing both the problems and the opportunities created by the introduction of high technology.
4. The churches should encourage by all possible means the exploration of alternative patterns of working and production, including the conversion of weapons production.

Participants

ADU, Mr A. Seth	Ghana	Ordinand
AMERY, Ms Lynne	England	Research and advisory work within local trade union, labour and community
ASHMALL, Mr Harry A.	Scotland	Headmaster; WCC Central and Executive Committees
ATKINSON, Rev. Richard	England	Anglican curate and Oxford Institute for Church and Society
ATKINSON, Mrs Helen	England	Materials scientist with UK Atomic Energy Authority
AUKES, Mr Tim	FRG	Sociologist (unemployed)
BONOW, Ms Ilse	FRG	Pastor in Duisburg
BARKER, Rev. Jonathan	Wales	Chaplain to sport and leisure, Diocese of Swansea and Brecon
BLEAKLEY, Rt Hon. David	Ireland	General Secretary, Irish Council of Churches
BUSH, Ms Alison	Scotland	Industrial youth chaplain in Glasgow
COLLSTE, Dr Göran	Sweden	University of Uppsala and Arbetsloshetsprojecktet. Swedish Ecumenical Council (not able to attend)
CRAIG, Rev. Maxwell	Scotland	Parish minister in Glasgow; convener of Church of Scotland Committee on Church and Nation
CRESSEY, Mr Peter	Scotland	Department of Social and Economic Research, University of Glasgow
CULLEN, Mrs Mary	Scotland	Chairwoman, Justice and Peace Commission, Glasgow
DARBY, Mr Jonathan	England	Quaker, teaching in microtechnology, University of Oxford, Department of External Studies

DAVIDSON, Mr John	Scotland	Scottish director, Confederation of British Industry
DODD, Rev. Charles	Australia	Industrial chaplain (Interchurch Trade and Industry Mission, Victoria)
DORRIS, Mr Tom	USA	Ecumenical Press Service, WCC
EDGE, Dr David	Scotland	Director, Science Studies Unit, University of Edinburgh
EKPENYONG, Rev. Udo	Nigeria	Training for industrial mission, Lagos
ELLINGTON, Mrs Kate	England	Project leader, secondary school Science Curriculum Review, Manchester
FYFE, Mr Walter	Scotland	Iona Community, urban worker in Glasgow
GURNEY, Mr Robin	England	WCC Commission of the Churches on International Affairs
HARVEY, Rev. John	Scotland	Parish minister, Govan, and various community employment projects
HULBERT, Mr Alastair	Scotland	Secretary, Scottish Churches Action for World Development (SCAWD)
KANE, Ms Margaret	England	Theological consultant to the churches and industrial mission in North East England
LAIDLAW, Mr Hugh	Scotland	Electronic design engineer, Glenrothes
LENDERS, Mr Marc	Belgium	ECCSEC, Brussels
LEUENBERGER, Prof. Dr Theodor	Switzerland	University of St Gallen
LYON, Dr David	England	Sociologist, Ilkley College, and convener of Shaftesbury Project, IT group
MAGERSTEDT, Dipl. Ing. Hansjurgen	GDR	Engineer; delegate of the Lutheran Church of Saxony; member of the board of Church and Society of the Evangelical Church
MATHEW, Mr Mohan	India	Project coordinator, International Youth Federation for Environmental Studies and Conservation; Member of the Church of South India

Participants

Macmillan, Mr David	Scotland	Unemployed
Maxwell, Mr Stephen	Scotland	Organizer, Scottish Education and Action for Development (SEAD)
Miner, Mr Maarten	Netherlands	Theology student
Moghbeli, Dr Fereydoun	Iran	Computer scientist, Glasgow College of Technology
Monaghan, Ms Anne	Scotland	Teacher, unemployed
Preston, Prof. Ronald	England	Department of Social and Pastoral Theology, University of Manchester
Ray, Rev. Cynthia	USA	Minister, Presbyterian Church
Ross, Rev. Donald	Scotland	Industrial mission organizer, Church of Scotland
Simpson, Prof. David	Scotland	Fraser of Allander Institute, University of Strathclyde
Smeall, Mr Ted	Scotland	Economist, Glasgow College of Technology
Smith, Mr J.B.	Scotland	Director, Ferranti plc. Edinburgh (recently retired)
Southern, Mr John	Wales	Quaker, Secretary of Industrial Committee, Council of Churches for Wales; part-time worker in cooperative enterprise
Stewart, Ms Ann	Scotland	Teacher of computing, Dalkeith
Thawng, Mr Smith Ngulh Za	Burma	Theologian, working among students
Walter, Dr Tony	England	Freelance writer, specializing in sociology
Whyte, Mr Robert	Scotland	Economic adviser, Manpower Services Commission
Williams, Sir Bruce, KBE	England	Director, The Technical Change Centre, London
Young, Councillor Ron	Scotland	Labour Group Secretary, Strathclyde Regional Council

Organizers

Davis, Dr Howard	Director, Society, Religion and Technology Project, Church of Scotland
Gosling, Dr David	Director, Church and Society, WCC

Bibliography

Selected publications in English which provide useful reviews and discussions for non-specialist audiences.

Employment trends

Roger Clarke, *Work in Crisis*, Saint Andrew Press, Edinburgh, 1982.

Charles Handy, *The Future of Work*, Blackwell, Oxford, 1985.

Ray Pahl, *Divisions of Labour*, Blackwell, Oxford, 1984.

New technology

Gunter Friedrichs and Adam Schaff, *Microelectronics and Society: for Better or for Worse*, Pergamon, Oxford and New York, 1982.

Peter Large, *The Micro Revolution Revised*, Pinter, 1984.

Judith K. Larsen and Everett M. Rogers, *Silicon Valley Fever*, Allen & Unwin, 1985.

David Lyon, *Future Society*, Lion Publishing, 1984.

The work ethic

Peter D. Anthony, *The Ideology of Work*, Tavistock, London, 1977.

Paul Ballard, *Towards a Contemporary Theology of Work*, Collegiate Centre of Theology, University College, Cardiff, 1984.

David Bleakley, *Work: the Shadow and the Substance*, SCM, London, 1983.

Michael Rose, *Reworking the Work Ethic*, Batsford, 1985.

Responses to unemployment

Church Action on Poverty, *Poverty Network* series of papers, Manchester.

Church Action with the Unemployed, *Action on Unemployment: 100 Projects with Unemployed People*, London, 1984.

Guy Dauncey, *The Unemployment Handbook*, National Extension College, 1982.

European Ecumenical Commission for Church and Society, *Unemployment and the Future of Work in the European Community*, Brussels, 1985.

Tony Walter, *Hope on the Dole*, SPCK, London, 1985.

Authors

Prof. THEODOR LEUENBERGER, Hochschule St Gallen für Wirtschafts- und Sozialwissenschaften, Switzerland

Sir BRUCE WILLIAMS, Director, The Technical Change Centre, London, UK

Prof. DAVID SIMPSON, Fraser of Allander Institute, University of Strathclyde, Scotland, UK

Mr JOHN DAVIDSON, Director, Confederation of British Industry (Scottish Office), UK

Ms LYNNE AMERY, Coventry Workshop, UK

Mr ROBERT WHYTE, Economic Adviser, Manpower Services Commission, UK

Mr MARC LENDERS, European Ecumenical Commission for Church and Society, Brussels, Belgium

Mr STEPHEN MAXWELL, Scottish Education and Action for Development, UK

Rt Hon. DAVID BLEAKLEY, General Secretary, Irish Council of Churches

Mr PETER CRESSEY, University of Glasgow, Scotland, UK

Dr GÖRAN COLLSTE, University of Uppsala, Sweden